the jacobites

the
jacobites

MOLLY DAVIDSON

GEDDES & GROSSET

Published 2004 by Geddes & Grosset,
David Dale House, New Lanark, ML11 9DJ, Scotland

ISBN 1 84205 354 X

Printed in Poland, OZGraf S.A.

Contents

Introduction

The word 'Jacobite' is derived from the Latin name 'Jacobus' – James – and was coined to refer to the supporters of James VII of Scotland and II of England, following the Glorious Revolution of 1688, when William of Orange and Mary came from Holland and took the thrones of Scotland, England and Ireland from him. In a broader sense, the term is used to refer to the supporters of the Stewart Dynasty, which finally lost its grip on the thrones of Great Britain when George I, elector of Hanover, succeeded Anne of Denmark in 1714.

There were – and there are still – people in Scotland, England, Ireland and many other countries who might be called 'true' Jacobites, in the strictest sense of the word. As far as these people were, and are concerned, Jacobitism is all about the Stewarts, rightful monarchs, wrongfully deposed. But the history of the Jacobites in Scotland – of all those who allied themselves with the Jacobite cause at any time – is more complicated than that.

The Stewart dynasty was a troubled one. Several Stewart monarchs died violent deaths. James I was murdered. James II was blown up by a cannon. James III was murdered after the battle of Sauchieburn and his son, James IV, killed on Flodden Field. Mary, Queen of Scots, was executed by Elizabeth I of England. Charles I lost his head after the Civil War. The Stewart monarchs from Robert II until James V had been almost constantly in conflict with England. Their lives were further blighted by struggles with, and between, powerful members of the nobility in Scotland and with constant unrest in the Highlands. The Reformation brought a different kind of threat to their hold on the throne. With the advent of Protestantism, the Stewart monarchs found themselves embroiled in an almost constant struggle with the Protestant Church. From the moment Mary, Queen of Scots, came to the throne in Scotland, her Roman Catholicism set her at odds with a large proportion of the population. Although Mary's son James was a Protestant, his resistance to the power of the Scottish Kirk preoccupied much of his time as king. The struggle with the Presbyterians in Scotland contributed directly to the downfall of Charles I and continued into the reign of Charles II.

Whether Catholic or Protestant, the Stewart monarchs believed that they had a hereditary divine right to rule and that rule extended to the Church. This meant having bishops, appointed by the king, in charge of the church; in the words of James VI and I, 'No bishop, no king'. And while the Anglican Protestants and Scottish Episcopalians accepted episcopacy, the extreme Protestants in Scotland continued to resist it. When James VII and II came to the thrones of Scotland and England, the conflict took on another aspect. The new king was Roman Catholic and actively sought to reinstate the rights of Roman Catholics in both Scotland and England. The threat of a return to the widely despised 'popery' caused deep resentment in both countries and was one of the principle factors that led to James's deposition and exile. It is fair to say that James VII and II lost his throne because of religious dissension. But those who sought to restore James VII and II to the thrones of Scotland, England and Ireland and his son to the throne of Great Britain did not do so necessarily for religious reasons. Some did, undoubtedly. Many Roman Catholics supported James, simply because he was a Catholic. The Episcopalians, of whom there were a great many in Scotland, also supported him, not only because he was leader of their church but also because they feared the rise of Presbyterianism and the repression of Episcopalianism. But the Jacobite rebellions were not simply religious conflicts.

The history of the Jacobites in Scotland, and in particular, of the rebellion of 1745, has been much romanticised. It is tempting to be persuaded by images of a proud and gallant nation struggling against the odds to try to restore its true sovereign to the throne, a nation left bereft by the loss of a monarch who had the God-given right to rule by hereditary succession. The heroic arrival of the young prince in 1745 with only seven loyal supporters, the brave clansmen thronging to his standard and the triumphant parades of Jacobite men proudly wearing white cockades in their bonnets through the streets of Edinburgh – it is all stirring stuff. The triumph of Prestonpans, when Johnny Cope was sent scuttling off to Berwick with his tail between his legs; the tragedy of Culloden, the slaughter of thousands of men and the death of the Jacobites' hopes; they are important events in the history of Scotland and their story is highly emotive. But the Jacobite rebellions were not the struggles of a nation.

In the first place, the Jacobite rebellions had an international dimension. They crossed the border into England and the sea to Ireland. The availability of military and financial support for the rebellions from abroad, in particular from France and Spain, played a crucial part in the successes and failures of successive risings.

In the second place, support for the Jacobite cause came from only a proportion of the Scottish population. The Scots did not rise as a nation for the Stewarts. Moreover, in Scotland as in England, support for the Jacobite cause was inconsistent. Those who came out in support of one rising did not necessarily support another. After 1707 and the union of the parliaments, a growing number of people became attracted to the Jacobite cause because they felt that Scotland should become independent again, and to some extent, therefore, the Jacobite cause became a nationalist cause. James Francis Edward tried to capitalise on Scottish nationalist feeling. The Declaration to the Scottish People, which he published shortly before his attempted invasion of Scotland in 1708, promised the Scots an independent parliament. Nonetheless, the Jacobite rebellions were not nationalist risings any more than they were religious risings.

The Jacobites were not a united body of people. Their aims and ideals were disparate. Their reasons for following the cause were varied. For some, it was religion, for others it was nationalism, but there were also those that followed for reasons of self-interest, for political power, or financial or personal security. Others followed out of loyalty, not necessarily to the Stewarts, but to their own leaders. The degree of commitment that those who professed to be Jacobite supporters were prepared to show to the cause also varied considerably. In many cases, loyalty to the cause came and went. Support for each successive rebellion depended very much on the political climate at the time, both nationally and internationally.

The rebellion of 1689 led by Viscount Dundee was almost a knee-jerk response to William of Orange's invasion. Dundee was one of those who firmly believed in King James's God-given right to rule. His support came from the Highlands and northeastern Lowlands, where many of the chiefs and landowners were Episcopalian or Roman Catholic. The chiefs had their own reasons for coming out to fight with Dundee, and not all of them were motivated only by a belief in the divine right of kings. Undoubtedly, for some, the conflict offered the chance to settle old scores in long-running clan feuds, in particular with the powerful, Protestant Campbells who supported the Williamite government. As far as the men of the clan were concerned, their first loyalty was to their chief, not the king. They were clansmen first and Jacobites second, if they considered themselves Jacobites at all. The rebellion in 1689 was supported by Louis XIV of France, but not on the Scottish front. Louis believed in the divine right of kings and consequently, believed that James's claim to be the rightful king of Scotland, England and Ireland was justified. Strictly speaking, therefore, Louis was a Jacobite. Louis supported James loyally in word, but not always in deed. It suited him to distract William from the conflict on the Continent and so he offered James troops for the invasion of Ireland, but the offer was made with the condition that the favour should be returned with Irish troops for France. French and other foreign aid for the Jacobite rebellions was always dependent upon the state of affairs in the wider arena.

The background to the failed rebellion of 1708 was substantially different to that of 1689. The Treaty of Union had been made and

Scotland was no longer an independent country. The Jacobites hoped to capitalise on the unpopularity of the union to raise support for a rebellion. In the event, it appeared that the people were not prepared for an uprising. The Highland clans, which Dundee had relied upon heavily and which were to be the backbone of the Jacobite forces in 1715 and 1745, were not brought into play. The French military, which Louis had provided for his own reasons, were unwilling to risk themselves without a wholehearted show of support from the British.

By 1715, the picture had changed again. Queen Anne had died. She, at least, had been a Stewart. The new king, George of Hanover, was not. The new king had excluded the Tories from his cabinet. Discontent with the union had grown considerably. Members of the nobility were feeling disempowered, and merchants had not yet reaped any significant benefits. More people were prepared to rise for the Jacobite cause – this time, many of them moved more by anti-union, anti-Hanoverian or anti-Whig sentiment than by pro-Stewart feelings. The surprise leader of the rising, the earl of Mar, had not been anti-union, nor had he demonstrated any loyalty to the Stewart dynasty up until 1715. It was only when he was deprived of a post in the government of George I that he took up the Jacobite standard. Mar's ability to change sides is particularly well known because he was the leader of the rebellion, but he was not the only one. The loyalty of many prominent people in Scotland to the Stewarts wavered, to say the least.

The final rebellion, in 1745, was sparked off by the frustration of Charles Edward Stewart at the failure of France to invade Great Britain on his father's behalf. Convinced that his appearance in Scotland would be enough to make all faithful Jacobites rise in a show of strength powerful enough to overthrow the Hanoverian monarchy, he embarked on his daring adventure across the sea. His accomplishments in the year that he spent in Britain were incredible, but the loyal Jacobites did not measure up to his expectations. There was a strong core of loyalty in the Highlands, but it was not as large as the prince might have hoped, or expected. Jacobite loyalty did not equate with blind obedience, as Charles found to his cost when his leaders overruled him. Moreover, Jacobite loyalty did not equate with willingness to commit. It took a great deal of persuasion to get the rebellion under way. At its largest, Charles's army was 8000 – a small proportion of the potential military might of the Highlands. It was also significantly smaller than the army that the earl of Mar raised in 1715. Support in Scotland was certainly far better than it was in England where hundreds – or thousands – of self-professed Jacobites refused to put their words into action for the prince. Nonetheless, it had dwindled. The reasons that some people might have had for following the cause had gone – either that, or they now had better reasons not to follow it. For some people, undoubtedly, Jacobitism was a lifelong commitment, enforced by strongly held beliefs. For others, Jacobitism was the lesser of two evils, a political strategy, a safety net or a flag of convenience.

For the Highlanders who took part in the Jacobite campaigns, Jacobitism was a duty. Because most of the fighting in the Jacobite rebellions took place in Scotland, people might be misled into thinking that Jacobite feelings were held most strongly by the Scots. But that is not the case. In 1689, while Dundee was leading the campaign in Scotland, thousands of Irish Jacobites were fighting in Ireland for King James. In the rebellions of 1715, 1719, and 1745, most of the fighting took place in Scotland and featured the Scots, but this was because it was only in the Scottish Highlands that large numbers of men could be easily be raised for a Jacobite army. Because of the ancient system of wardholding, whereby land was granted in exchange for military service, the clansmen of the Highlands were under a legal obligation to serve as soldiers to their chiefs. The landowners in England had no such powers over their tenants. Whereas a Jacobite clan chief could raise hundreds of men to his service, the English noble could only hope to persuade his tenants to join him. It was a case of collective duty, versus individual choice. If the Highlanders had not been under an obligation to serve their chiefs, it is doubtful whether the Scots Jacobites could have mustered any more, or even as many, men as the English Jacobites did. The plotting, the planning, the espionage and the intrigue would still have gone on, in Scotland, England, France and elsewhere, but without the men of the Jacobite clans, the risings would not have happened.

The full history of the Jacobites is extremely complicated. From the arrival of William of Orange to the death of Charles Edward Stewart, it spans the reigns of four British sovereigns, and involves both the internal politics and foreign policies of several countries. This book deals primarily with the Scottish Jacobites, but their story stretches far beyond the confines of Scotland. The Scottish Jacobites were only part of a movement that had followers all over Great Britain and on the Continent. They were also, sometimes, pawns in the games of the major European powers. It is important to try to understand the story of the Scottish Jacobites as part of a wider picture. But it is equally important to be able to take a closer view, to recognise what the struggles meant on a more personal level for those who took part in the rebellions. Armies went here, ships went there, battles were fought and won or lost; it is easy to get caught up in the manoeuvres, the strategies, the chronology of events. But what should never be forgotten is that all these events involved men having to leave their families and homes, to fight for a cause they possibly did not understand. These men endured extremes of hunger, cold, pain and fatigue. They marched hundreds of miles across difficult and dangerous terrain, in all weathers, following their leaders. They fought in desperate, bloody and brutal battles, sometimes knowing that they were likely to die. When the fighting was over, many faced imprisonment, transportation or execution. The history of the Jacobite rebellions is fascinating. But the bravery, resilience and stamina of the fighting men make the closer view particularly remarkable.

Timeline

1673
20 September: James, duke of York, marries Mary of Modena by proxy. The marriage vows are taken in person on 21 November.

1676
James, duke of York, converts to Roman Catholicism.

1685
6 February: Charles II dies.
23 April: James II is crowned.

1688
10 June: birth of James Francis Edward, son of James VII and Mary of Modena.
5 November: William of Orange lands in England.
22 December: James VII leaves for France.

1689
13 February: a convention at Westminster declares the English throne vacant.
14 March: the Convention of the Estates meets in Scotland, claims the right to declare the throne vacant and offers it to William of Orange.
March: Viscount Dundee moves north to rally support for James and the first Jacobite insurrection begins.
24 March: James VII arrives in Ireland.
11 April: William and Mary are crowned king and queen of England.

27 July: the battle of Killiecrankie. The Jacobites defeat General
  Mackay's forces. Viscount Dundee is killed.
July: Edinburgh Castle, held by the duke of Gordon for the Jacobites,
  submits.
21 August: the battle of Dunkeld.

1690
1 May: Jacobite forces under General Buchan are defeated in a surprise attack at Cromdale.
1 July: James is defeated by William of Orange at the battle of the
  Boyne.

1691
Jacobite supporters take possession of the Bass Rock in the Forth.

1692
13 February: the massacre of Glencoe.

1694
April: Jacobites on the Bass Rock surrender.
28 December: Queen Mary dies.

1695
The Scots parliament passes an act establishing the Company of
  Scotland, trading to Africa and the East Indies.

1697
The War of the Grand Alliance ends with the Treaty of Ryswick –
  Louis XIV agrees to recognise William of Orange as king of
  England.

1701
September: James VII dies. Louis XIV proclaims James's son,
  James Francis Edward, as king of England, Scotland and Ireland.
The Act of Settlement is passed by the English parliament.

1702
8 March: William of Orange dies. Anne of Denmark becomes
  queen.

Hostilities break out between England and France in the War of the Spanish Succession.

1703–04

The Act Anent Peace and War, the Wine Act and the Act of Security are passed by the Scots parliament.

1705

The Aliens Act is passed by the English parliament.

1707

March: the Treaty of Union is signed.

1708

Failed rebellion attempt by the Jacobite supporters. James VIII, sponsored by Louis XIV, attempts a landing in Scotland but the French fleet is forced back.

1710

The Tories come to power in Great Britain and Jacobite hopes rise.

1713

The Treaty of Utrecht. James Francis Edward is forced under the terms of the treaty to leave France.

1714

July: Sophia, electress of Hanover, dies. George, elector of Hanover, is now first in line to succeed Anne to the British throne.

Oxford is dismissed from parliament and the Whig earl of Shrewsbury is selected by Anne to replace him.

1 August: Queen Anne dies. George of Hanover is proclaimed king.

18 September: George I lands at Greenwich.

20 October: George I is crowned at Westminster.

1715

March: the Whigs take control in the new parliament of George I. Viscount Bolingbroke flees to France.

July: the duke of Ormonde, nominated leader of the rebellion in the southwest of England, flees to France. Parliament suspends the Habeas Corpus Act.

1 August: the earl of Mar sets out for Scotland to rally the clans for the Jacobite cause.

21 August: Louis XIV dies.

6 September: Mar raises the Jacobite standard at Braemar.

14 September: Colonel John Hay takes Perth for the Jacobites. The duke of Argyll arrives in Edinburgh to command Hanoverian forces in Scotland.

28 September: Mar enters Perth.

September–October: the rising in the southwest of England is crushed.

7 October: King James III is proclaimed at Warkworth by Forster and the Northumbrian Jacobites.

12–13 October: Mackintosh of Borlum crosses the Forth with his troops.

18 October: King James is proclaimed in Jedburgh by Kenmuir and the Border Jacobites.

19 October: Kenmuir and Forster join forces.

22 October: Mackintosh of Borlum's force joins up with those of Forster and Viscount Kenmuir at Kelso.

9 November: the cavalry of the Jacobite force under Forster enter Preston.

13 November: the battle of Sherriffmuir. After an indecisive battle, the earl of Mar claims victory.

14 November: the English Jacobites surrender at Preston.

22 December: James Francis Edward, the Pretender, arrives in Scotland, at Peterhead.

24 December: the earl of Derwentwater and Viscount Kenmuir are executed.

1716

January: the Pretender reaches Perth.

31 January: the Jacobite army moves north.

4 February: the Pretender and the earl of Mar leave Scotland.

Mid-February: the Jacobite army disperses.

A Disarming Act is passed.

1719

May–June: attempt at another rising with Spanish support.

10 June: Jacobite forces are defeated at the battle of Glenshiel by General Wightman.

13 September: James Francis Edward marries Clementina Sobieska in Italy.

1720

31 December: birth of Charles Edward Stewart, son of James Francis Edward and Clementina Sobieska.

1727

George I dies and George II comes to the throne.

1740

War of Austrian Succession breaks out.

1744

February: an attempt to restore the Stewarts to the throne with French support is scuppered when the French invasion fleet is damaged by storms before setting off from France.

1745

June: Charles Edward Stewart sets off from France with two ships.

July: Charles lands on Eriskay with the Seven Men of Moidart.

25 July: Charles lands on the mainland at Borrodale.

19 August: the Jacobite standard is raised at Glenfinnan.

4 September: the Jacobite army under Charles Edward Stewart enters Perth.

17 September: the Jacobite army enters Edinburgh.

21 September: Jacobite victory against government forces under Sir John Cope at Prestonpans.

3 November: the advance into England begins.

16 November: the Jacobite army proclaims James III at Carlisle.

24–25 November: the Jacobite army enters Preston.

6 December: the Jacobite army turns back from Derby and begins the march back north.

20 December: the Jacobite army crosses the border into Scotland.

25December: the Jacobite army enters Glasgow.

1746

3 January: the Jacobite army leaves Glasgow.

17 January: the battle of Falkirk. The Jacobite army defeats government troops led by General Hawley. The withdrawal into the Highlands begins.

16 April: the Jacobite army is defeated at the battle of Culloden Moor. The survivors flee and Charles goes into hiding.

17 April: Lord George Murray writes a letter of resignation to Charles from Ruthven Barracks.

20 April: Charles writes to his chiefs informing them that he will be leaving for France and telling them to disperse.

20 September: Charles escapes to France.

1766

James Francis Edward Stewart dies.

1788

31 January: Charles Edward Stewart dies.

CHAPTER ONE

The Accession of James VII

James might never have become king of England. During later years of the reign of his brother, Charles II, anti-Catholic sentiment was running high in England. Charles himself was not a Roman Catholic (although he converted to Catholicism shortly before his death), but his tolerance of Catholics was deeply unpopular with the English parliament, which was dominated by Whigs. When James, duke of York, Charles's brother, chose the Catholic Mary of Modena as his second wife in 1673, there was widespread unease. The duke's conversion to Catholicism in 1676 caused further disruption. As King Charles had no living heirs, James was his successor to the throne. The prospect of a Catholic monarch was not welcomed by many. There was a move by the Whigs to pass an Exclusion Bill in 1679, denying the right of Roman Catholics to rule and effectively barring James from succeeding his brother. Charles responded by dissolving parliament. Fortunately for James, by the time Charles II died, there was a Tory majority in parliament once again, which was more favourably disposed to his succession. In 1685, James came to the throne of Scotland, England and Ireland.

James had made his presence felt in Scotland before he became king. As duke of Albany, he had played a major role in the persecution of the Covenanters. When he came to the throne, the 'Killing Time' was at its peak. Government troops were breaking up conventicles and hunting down the rebellious Covenanters who refused to accept the sovereign's right to take charge of the affairs of the Church. Although Roman Catholicism was still illegal,

Episcopalianism had been re-established. The Scots of the Protestant Church were being forced to accept the leadership of bishops appointed with royal approval rather than leaders appointed by themselves and this was deeply resented by many. The Episcopal Church was strong in Scotland, particularly in the northeast. Additionally, several of the clan chiefs in the Highlands were Episcopalian. But there was a strong body of opinion in Scotland, particularly among the Presbyterians of southern Lowlands, that was strongly opposed to the idea of royal supremacy over the affairs of the Church. The pro-Catholic measures that James introduced after he came to the throne further antagonised a great many Scots. Although the Presbyterians were granted freedom of worship by the king's Letter of Indulgence of July 1686, they suspected that James was moving towards imposing Catholic supremacy.

It was in England, however, that James's growing unpopularity led to his downfall.

When Charles died in 1685, he had left the monarchy in a stronger position, both financially and politically, than it had been for many years. If James had ruled with the same principles as his brother had done, and if he had not moved to promote the interests of the Roman Catholic Church with the enthusiasm that he did, he might have retained his hold on the throne. As it was, in three short years he had managed to undo all the good that had been achieved by Charles.

CHAPTER TWO

The Glorious Revolution: the Struggle Begins

Within months of his succession to the throne, James had begun to antagonise the English parliament. In the autumn of 1685, he began making financial demands, to fund substantial increases in his standing army. He also asked for a repeal of the Test Acts which had barred Roman Catholics from holding public office so that he could employ Catholic officers in prominent positions in the military. Parliament refused, but in the following year, following a court case which found in his favour, James began placing Roman Catholics in high positions in both the army and the Church. These moves provoked deep suspicion that James intended to enforce Roman Catholicism on the country.

On 4 April, 1687, James issued a Declaration of Indulgence, pledging religious toleration. Although the terms of the declaration included not only Roman Catholics but also dissenters, English Protestants viewed it with deep suspicion, seeing it as another move to promote the interests and increase the power of the Roman Catholics over them. On 27 April 1688, a second Declaration of Indulgence was issued, reiterating the terms of the first. On 4 May, the king gave out an order that the declaration was to be read out in every church in the country. The bishops of seven dioceses refused to comply with the order, and the king had them arrested. The bishops were brought to trial on 29 June 1688, but they were acquitted on 30 June.

James's marriage to the Roman Catholic Mary Beatrice of Modena was unpopular, but it was tolerated, partly due to the fact that it seemed that the couple would be unable to produce a live heir. From

1674 to 1684, Mary had given birth to ten children, but five of them had been stillborn and the other five had not survived beyond early infancy. James had two surviving children, Mary and Anne, by his first marriage to Anne Hyde and both of them were Protestants. As long as James's marriage to Mary of Modena failed to produce an heir, Mary and Anne were first and second in line to succeed him. In June 1688, when a healthy son was at last born to the king and his wife, it is not surprising that stories were spread that the child was not Mary of Modena's, but had been smuggled into the palace in a warming-pan. The birth of the baby, named James Francis Edward, effectively sealed the king's fate. The prospect of a Roman Catholic heir to the throne was intolerable to the English. A plan was put in place to remedy the situation. At the end of June, the Protestant ruler of the Netherlands, William of Orange, husband of James's elder daughter, Mary, was invited by prominent English parliamentarians to come over to England and take the throne from James.

Initially, James did not seem to take the threat seriously, but by September, he was convinced that his position was in jeopardy. He sent orders to Scotland that the principal castles of Edinburgh and Stirling were to be provisioned in preparation for their defence. Word was sent out to the chiefs of the Highland clans that they were to be prepared to call up their men in support of the king at short notice. Meanwhile, the soldiers of the regular army were to be assembled and brought to England under the command of Lieutenant-General James Douglas and Major-General Graham of Claverhouse, to reinforce his army there. More than fifty ships of the English navy were stationed off the southwest coast to prevent William of Orange from making a landing.

In November 1688, successfully evading all the naval defences put in place by the king, William landed at Torbay with an army of 14,000 men. Although much of the country was ready to welcome his arrival, the reception he got in the southwest, which was largely loyal to the king, was hostile. If James had acted decisively at this stage, he might have been able to repel the invasion successfully.

After hearing of William's landing, James gave orders for most of his army to move from London to Salisbury, leaving a small force behind to defend the capital. He followed on some days later. His delay had cost him. A number of his senior officers in the English army, including Churchill and General Kirk, were ready to defect. Feeling that he could not proceed without the loyalty of his entire force, James decided to withdraw the army behind the Thames. He left the army there and returned to London, where he made the decision to leave for France, where he had already made arrangement for his wife and baby son to be safely transported. The king's decision not to continue with an offensive against William of Orange was greeted with dismay by the leaders of his Scottish army, in particular Graham of Claverhouse, now Viscount Dundee, but he could not be persuaded otherwise.

James's first attempt at flight was unsuccessful. He was captured at the coast and brought back to London. His loyal supporters made a second attempt to persuade him to stay and fight for his throne but were again unsuccessful. He departed once more, after having appointed Dundee commander of his army in Scotland and placed Colin, earl of Balcarres, in charge of civil affairs. This time, William of Orange, who could see the obvious advantages to his own position if James were seen to abdicate, ensured that his passage to Rochester was unhindered. On 22 December 1688, James sailed for France, accompanied by his illegitimate son, the duke of Berwick. He landed at Ambleteuse on Christmas day and from there travelled to the Palace of St Germain which the French king had put at his disposal.

CHAPTER THREE

John Graham of Claverhouse

John Graham of Claverhouse, son of William Graham of Claverhouse, a noble from Angus of royal descent, was born in 1643. Educated at St Andrews University, he excelled as a soldier in France and Holland before returning to Scotland in 1677 to serve Charles II. He was a prominent figure in the campaign to suppress the Covenanters and his activities in this respect earned him the unenviable nickname of 'Bluidy Clavers'. He continued to serve as a military leader in the reign of James VII and II and became Viscount Dundee in 1688. He was a capable and charismatic military leader and demonstrated a loyalty to his king that was not equalled by any of his peers.

When William of Orange landed in England, Dundee was already in England, in command of a company of horse in the Scottish army. He and the earl of Balcarres urged the king to lead an army to face William and assert his position as rightful ruler, but in vain. Determined that Scotland should not submit to the usurper's rule as easily as England had, Dundee urged royal sympathisers in Scotland to remain strong in their resolve to resist William of Orange's attempts to take the Scottish throne.

Unfortunately, although Edinburgh Castle still held out as a stronghold loyal to the king under the command of the duke of Gordon, the situation elsewhere in the capital city had changed for the worse. The absence of the regular army and the king's most powerful supporters from the capital had left the way clear for the Whigs to take control. Dundee stayed in England for some time after the king's departure. When he heard of the forthcoming

Convention of the Estates in Edinburgh, being held to consider whether Scotland should follow England's lead and reject King James in favour of the prince from Holland, Dundee travelled north. On his arrival, he found that the mood in the capital was far from supportive of the king. A large number of Whigs from the southwest had come into Edinburgh for the Convention. Many of them held bitter feelings of enmity, not only towards King James, but also towards Dundee. Following the events of the 'Glorious Revolution' in England, there had been serious disruptions in the capital and elsewhere in the Lowlands. A mob had broken into the Catholic Chapel Royal at Holyrood and destroyed it. In the south-west of Scotland, Episcopalian ministers were being driven from their parishes by angry mobs of Presbyterians.

Confronted by a clearly Whig majority at the Convention of the Estates, Dundee was at once convinced that the king's position in Scotland could not be saved by political means, and resolved to seek a military solution to the problem. He could expect little or no support from the south of Scotland. Remaining in Edinburgh, where his life was in danger and where nothing could be done for King James, was not an option. Dundee knew that his hopes for restoring James to the throne lay in the Highlands and in the northeast of Scotland. Accordingly, he left Edinburgh and headed north.

CHAPTER FOUR

The Irish Campaign,
March 1689–July 1690

While Viscount Dundee was rallying support for his king in Scotland, James was making his own plans for a comeback.

The fugitive King James was given a warm welcome by Louis XIV. The Palace of St Germain provided ample accommodation for the exiled Jacobite court and the French king awarded James a generous pension. Almost as soon as James arrived in France, he began negotiations with Louis as to how the thrones of Scotland, England and Ireland might be regained with his help.

Louis was prepared to assist, but his willingness to offer his support involved self-interest as well as generosity. William's new role as king of Scotland and England meant an alliance of military power between Holland and Britain, which posed a considerable threat to France's status as a major power. Whether or not an invasion of Ireland was likely to succeed in restoring James to his throne, Louis could see the value of destabilising William's position in Britain. Conflict in Britain would prevent William from engaging all his troops on the Continent, where the French army was threatening the interests of the Dutch and other members of the Grand Alliance. At the beginning of 1689, Louis agreed to supply James with a force of French troops for an invasion of Ireland. There was strong Jacobite support in Ireland, where a large proportion of the people were still Roman Catholic. The Lord Deputy, the earl of Tyrconnel, was a Catholic and loyal to James and, under Tyrconnel's control, most of the country had also kept its allegiance. Support for James was strong in the south of Ireland and also in a large part of Ulster. It was James's intention to consolidate his position in

Ireland before turning his attentions to Scotland. He was in communication with Viscount Dundee and gave him his word that as
soon as the manpower could be spared, troops would be on their
way from Ireland to support the Scottish rising.

Preparations were made swiftly for the invasion of Ireland and on
22 March, the expedition finally got under way. James arrived in
Dublin on 24 March.

James wanted to secure control of all of Ireland before William
of Orange sent a force over from England to oppose him. Resistance to the Jacobites was centred in Enniskillen and in Derry,
where the gates had been closed against a Catholic garrison sent by
Tyrconnel in December 1688.

James went to Derry himself in April, optimistic that the citizens
could be persuaded to surrender, but it quickly became clear that
both Derry and Enniskillen would resist to the last. He left his illegitimate son, the duke of Berwick, in charge of operations in the north
and returned to the south. Derry and Enniskillen were major
stumbling-blocks to the progress of James's long-term plans. As long
as they held out against the Jacobite forces, James could not release
the troops he had promised for Dundee's campaign in Scotland.
Furthermore, as long as James was deprived of overall control of
Ulster, communication lines between Ireland and Scotland were in
jeopardy.

There was a very large force inside Derry, larger than the Jacobite
army that was surrounding it. The number of people within the
city walls had been increased considerably by Protestant soldiers
and inhabitants of the areas around Derry who had sought refuge
within the city walls. Conditions were crowded and insanitary, but
the people remained confident in their defiance. The people of
Enniskillen were equally troublesome. Parties of attackers from the
town were continually harassing the Jacobite troops with no small
degree of success.

Derry held out against the Jacobites until 28 July, when three English ships broke through the booms on the River Foyle to bring
relief to the city. The Jacobite army withdrew. On the same day, a
Jacobite army sent from Dublin under the command of Viscount

Mountcashel was defeated at Newtonbutler, with devastating loss of life, by an army of Williamites from Enniskillen. This defeat led to the withdrawal of Jacobite forces from most of Ulster.

On 13 August 1689, William's army, led by Marshal Schomberg, landed in County Down as the last of the Jacobite forces were withdrawing to the south. Schomberg got as far as Dundalk, where a force led by Tyrconnel made a stand against his army, blocking progress to Dublin. No battle was fought and the situation remained in stalemate for the winter. In spring, both William's army and James's army were reinforced – James's by French troops and William's by English and Dutch. On 14 June 1690, William landed in Ireland. At the head of an army of more than 35,000 men, he moved south and, on 1 July, defeated James's army at the battle of the Boyne. Five days later, William entered Dublin. James, realising that the cause was lost, soon sailed back to France. Although the Catholics in the south continued to resist and there was no formal surrender until the Treaty of Limerick in 1691, the Jacobite campaign in Ireland was effectively over. In Scotland too, where Jacobites had long waited for military support from Ireland, the last faint hope of challenging William had gone.

CHAPTER FIVE

Dundee's Campaign, 1689

After his departure from Edinburgh in March 1689, Viscount Dundee became a hunted man. The duke of Hamilton, president of the Convention of Estates, sensing the danger of an insurrection in favour of James, ordered the arrest of both Dundee and the earl of Balcarres. Balcarres was captured and imprisoned in Edinburgh, but Dundee remained at large. From Edinburgh, Dundee first travelled to his seat at Dudhope. He raised the Jacobite standard on Dundee Law before heading north, to the Highlands, to rally support.

The Convention of the Estates was swift to react. In response to the threat from Dundee, they made preparations for effective military opposition. Major-General Hugh Mackay had been appointed commander of all forces in Scotland by William and Mary. He was now put in command of more than 1000 men of the Scotch Brigade, newly arrived from Holland. These troops were reinforced by a body of horse commanded by Sir Patrick Hume, 800 infantry under the command of the earl of Leven, and 200 dragoons who were sent from England.

For the next two and a half months, an elaborate game of cat and mouse was played out by Dundee and Mackay.

Dundee was not ready for military action. He had brought only a small group of loyal cavalry back from England with him. There was little, if any, support for him amongst the ranks of the nobility in Edinburgh. Even those who supported the principle that James should still be king were unwilling to show their hands at this stage. The duke of Gordon, one of the few whose loyalty was unquestionable, was showing his resistance to the revolution by holding

Edinburgh Castle and could not be persuaded to abandon that course of action and follow Dundee. Before Dundee could contemplate taking on the comparative might of Mackay's force, he had to enlist the help of the Highland chieftains loyal to James. By April, he had word that James had reached Dublin and that as soon as the Jacobite position in Ireland was secure, a substantial body of troops would be sent to Scotland to support the rebellion. Dundee was optimistic that this would happen relatively soon. In order to buy time to bring his force up to full strength, Dundee had to keep a constant eye on Mackay's movements and steer a path that avoided a premature encounter.

While Dundee moved north into Aberdeenshire to recruit vassals of the duke of Gordon, Mackay set off from Edinburgh and established a headquarters for his army at Dundee. A portion of his army remained in Edinburgh, laying siege to the castle. Mackay then left a company of dragoons at Dundee under the command of Lieutenant-Colonel Livingstone and advanced north at the head of approximately 500 men.

Mackay had got as far as Brechin, when he heard that Dundee was on his way back south and was only a few miles to the north of him. Dundee, having heard that Livingstone's dragoons were contemplating coming over to the Jacobite army, was hurrying back to his home town in the hope of recruiting them. Mackay was hopeful of catching Dundee but was too late. Hearing of Mackay's approach, Dundee hastily changed his plans and turned back to the north.

Mackay then headed into Aberdeenshire in pursuit of Dundee. He followed him from Aberdeenshire into Moray, where he learned that Dundee had crossed the Spey without opposition and had moved on to Inverness. At Inverness, Dundee's army, which had amounted to a little over 150 horse, was increased by approximately 1000 Macdonalds under Macdonald of Keppoch. Mackay's force was now considerably smaller than Dundee's. He feared that Dundee would now seek out an encounter with him. He moved to Elgin and sent out messages to loyal landowners in the district, demanding reinforcements.

Eventually, having been joined by reinforcements of horse, and with the promise of several hundred infantry to come, Mackay ventured north from Elgin towards Inverness, which Dundee had already vacated. At Inverness, 500 more men joined up with him – Mackays from Sutherland, Grants from Strathspey and Rosses. Mackay sent a message south to Edinburgh for further reinforcements from the Dutch regiments under the command of Colonel Ramsay.

Dundee was also preoccupied with recruiting. Having sent out messages to chiefs loyal to the Stewart cause, he arranged for them to muster at Lochaber on 18 May. He then moved into Atholl. While the marquis of Atholl had shown no wish to take any active part in rebellion against William and remained in Edinburgh, the men of Atholl were less reticent and were very welcoming to Dundee. From Atholl, Dundee conducted a surprise raid on Perth, where government troops were being raised, seized a large amount of money that had been collected as tax from the revenue office and captured four officers and thirty horses. After recruiting more cavalry in Angus, he set off for the meeting with the clansmen at Lochaber. At Lochaber, he was joined by more than 1500 men – Macdonalds of Morar, Glencoe and Keppoch, Stewarts of Appin, Camerons and Clanranald's men.

Meanwhile, things were not going so well for Mackay. Ramsay's troops were delayed in setting off from Edinburgh. A fleet of boats had been spotted in the River Forth and there had been fears that it was a French invasion force. Ramsay was forced to keep his force in the capital until it was at last discovered that the 'French' boats were only fishing boats from Holland.

When Ramsay's force finally left Edinburgh, they moved north through Perth into Atholl and towards Ruthven. The reception that greeted the government troops in Atholl was alarmingly hostile and Ramsay's determination faltered. Then the news came that Dundee, having moved back east from Lochaber, had placed himself between Ramsay's force and Mackay's army in Inverness. Ramsay decided to withdraw back to Perth. Mackay was on his way to meet Ramsay at Ruthven when he heard of the withdrawal and of Dundee's presence in the vicinity. Mackay at once headed for

Strathspey, with Dundee following. Ruthven was seized by Dundee's
men, the garrison was captured and the fortress destroyed. Mackay
prepared for battle in Strathspey, but Dundee was still unwilling to
risk such a commitment at this stage. A day was spent with the two
sides sizing each other up, each sending parties out to check on the
other's position, before Mackay continued his retreat to south of
the River Bogie, where he made camp. The next day, Mackay's
army was reinforced by two regiments under the command of
Barclay and Leslie who had come from the south. The additional
men gave him renewed confidence and he turned back on his
tracks, towards Dundee's army. Now it was Dundee's army that
was retreating. Mackay's force secured victory in a minor skirmish
with a body of men who were on their way to join Dundee's army,
killing around 80 men at a cost of only 7 dead of their own men,
and continued the pursuit of Dundee as far as Badenoch. En route,
they were finally joined by Ramsay's regiment, which had moved
north again while Dundee and Mackay were in Strathspey.

Dundee withdrew to Lochaber and Mackay gave up the chase
and moved back to Inverness. He sent detachments of his army to
Strathbogie and Elgin to hold these areas for the government. He
also sent a message to the duke of Hamilton in Edinburgh, asking
for the wheels to be set in motion for the building of a fortress at
Inverlochy in Lochaber, which was to be manned by a garrison of
several hundred men. A strong government presence in this region
would hopefully keep the rebellious Highlanders subdued.
Braemar was also to be garrisoned, but the dragoons sent to carry
out that task were taken by surprise by a party of Jacobites and the
house at Braemar was torched. A small garrison was left at
Abergeldie and more troops were posted further down the Dee.

By this time, Mackay had received news that following his return
to Lochaber, Dundee had dismissed a large part of his Highland
army. Mackay now felt, as the smaller garrisons were now in place
at their new posts, it was safe to return to Edinburgh, to push
through the plans for the establishment of the fort at Inverlochy.

When Mackay reached Edinburgh, he was extremely disappointed and frustrated to find that nothing had been done to start

building fortifications at Inverlochy, nor was much willingness shown to proceed with the plan after his arrival. Time was running out if the fort was to be built, provisioned and garrisoned with a sizeable force before the winter set in. Morale in the capital was low. The Jacobites were in control of all of Ireland, with the exception of two cities. It was feared that members of the Scottish nobility who had previously refrained from committing to either side were on the verge of siding with the Jacobites. Moreover, there were strong signs of discontent with the Williamite government in England as well.

Mackay felt that it was imperative to strengthen the government's position in the area north of the Tay in order to prevent the rebellion from spreading further south, but it seemed there were neither the funds nor the men available for his plans. The conflict in Ireland was now preoccupying the king and a great many of his troops and no more could be spared.

Dundee had also had his disappointments. He had waited for more than two months for the troops that King James had promised to send from Ireland. The troops that finally did arrive on the west coast to join him amounted to only a few hundred foot soldiers, commanded by Colonel Cannon. Their provision ships had been captured by English frigates off the Western Isles. The men were hardly trained and badly equipped. Nonetheless, Dundee's optimism was boosted when he learned that the tenants on the estates of Atholl, disregarding the fact that their landlord, the marquis of Atholl, was siding with the government, had taken control of Blair Castle for the Jacobites.

CHAPTER SIX

The Battle of Killiecrankie,
27 July 1689

Mackay had also heard the news that Blair Castle had been taken. He abandoned his plans for an advance into Lochaber and set off for Stirling, before moving to Perth, where he had ordered his troops to assemble, and on towards Atholl. Dundee, meanwhile, sent messages out to rally the Jacobite clansmen again and began to march east from Lochaber. By the time Mackay reached Perth, Dundee was in Badenoch and leading the vanguard of his army towards Atholl.

Mackay continued his journey with all speed. His army numbered around 4500 men. His intention was to try to recapture Blair Castle before Dundee reached it. On 26 July, his army had reached Dunkeld, where they made camp for the night.

Lord Murray, son of the duke of Murray, had gone to Atholl some days before Mackay's advance from Edinburgh, to try to recover Blair Castle from his father's rebellious tenants. His efforts were no avail. Realising that Dundee was marching through Atholl towards Blair, he abandoned Blair and retreated back to join Mackay. Between Mackay's position in Dunkeld and Dundee at Blair lay the Pass of Killiecrankie, running from just south of Blair towards Pitlochry. Murray posted men at the northern end of the pass to try to prevent Dundee from advancing further.

The next morning, Mackay led his army out of Dunkeld very early in the morning and proceeded towards the narrow pass. Hearing of Mackay's advance, Dundee was forced to make a quick decision. His hasty march from Lochaber had been made without some of the clans who made up a large portion of his army. They were still on their way to Blair. Mackay's force at this stage outnumbered his own almost two to one. In spite of these unfavourable odds, Dundee decided that he should go ahead with a battle, rather than risk having to make an ignominious retreat while he waited for the rest of his men to arrive. The outcome of the forthcoming conflict would depend on Dundee's skills as a military strategist.

The Pass of Killiecrankie was narrow and confined. An ambush could be carried out while Mackay's army was still in the pass, but a move into the pass would place Dundee's at considerable risk, as escape would be difficult. The best outcome of an ambush at the northern end of the pass would probably be the destruction of only a small part of Mackay's force, while the rest would be able to retreat back through the pass.

Dundee calmly allowed Mackay to continue his progress through the pass and assemble his army at the northern end. The River Garry, which runs through the pass, turns northwest at this point. On its bank to the northwest is a stretch of comparatively level ground, overlooked by the slopes of a steep hill. Here was where the general stopped his army. Dundee sent a party of men from Blair, following the course of the River Garry towards Killiecrankie, as a diversion. This was the direction from where Mackay expected the attack to come. The main body of Dundee's army, however, was taken from Blair to the east across the River Tilt and then round the high ground to the northeast of the pass. Crossing a small stream, the Alt Chluain, which runs down to the River Tilt from the high ground, they then came southwest down the gully of the stream a short distance before turning to the southeast again and appearing on the slopes of the hill above Mackay's army.

Mackay had assembled his army in battle formation, facing along the course of the River Garry in the direction of Blair. When he realised that, contrary to his expectations, Dundee's men were drawing up on the hillside to his right, he immediately gave the order for

his army to do a quarter turn to face them. He then moved them up
from the river to a stretch of comparatively level ground some distance up the hill. Dundee still had the advantage of higher ground,
but Mackay had the advantage of far superior numbers. Dundee
distributed his men as far as possible across the hillside, clansmen
grouped in their clan formations to the left and right, horse in the
centre. Some time was spent by both armies manoeuvring from
side to side, trying to place themselves in the most advantageous
position. Dundee's main concern, having the smaller force, was
that Mackay's army would be able to outflank him and launch an
attack from the sides as well as from the front. Mackay, for his part,
was anxious that Dundee should not move round his right flank
and cut off the entrance to the pass, and access to Perth. He spread
out his troops as thinly as possible, in a long line only three deep, to
counter this threat. Neither of the two armies placed any men in
the rear as reserve. For two hours, the armies manoeuvred and
waited.

Mackay began the offensive with some ineffective artillery fire,
then gave his men the order to fire their muskets. The first row
fired, then stepped to the side and back to let the men behind
them come forward to take their turn, thus keeping up a steady
volley of shots. There was little return of fire from the Highlanders. They stood on the hillside above, biding their time a little
longer. At last, as the sun was sinking, the Highlanders began to
move forward down the hill, crouching low, sometimes flat on
their stomachs with their targes held in front to protect them from
the shots fired by Mackay's army. Many Jacobites were killed as
they moved forward, but nothing would stop the advance. They
moved steadily and surely downhill until they were less than 100
yards from the enemy and then they discharged their muskets. As
soon as they had fired, they threw the muskets aside and charged,
broadsword in hand, upon the government troops. The swiftness
of the Highland charge and the terror which it struck in the hearts
of their opponents were always what made it particularly lethal
and the charge at Killiecrankie was no exception. Few of Mackay's

men had time to fire more than a single volley at the horde of clansmen thundering down the hill. Many of them were still fumbling with their bayonets, trying to screw them into the end of their muskets, when the Highlanders fell upon them, slashing into their lines with their broadswords. Dundee charged with his horsemen into the middle of the throng to attack Mackay's cavalry. The right wing of Mackay's army held out for a little longer than the left, but only a little. The sheer shock of the Highland charge had thrown his troops into complete confusion. Mackay tried to rally his cavalry to attack the right and left flanks of the Highlanders, who were concentrating their efforts against his infantry on the centre, but they did not follow his orders. After an initial advance, they turned, causing further chaos amongst the ranks of infantry.

The battle did not last long. More than 1200 men on the government side were killed in the initial onslaught, while several hundred more met their deaths trying to escape across the River Garry or back through the Pass of Killiecrankie. Mackay managed to gather a few hundred horsemen and they made good their escape across the River Garry and to the west. The Jacobites still on the field had by this time turned their efforts to plundering the remnants of Mackay's baggage train and did not take up the pursuit. The victory had been a decisive one for the Jacobites. Nonetheless, their losses were substantial. Several hundred men lay dead on the battlefield, most of them having been felled by musket fire as they made their first advance downhill. More importantly, Viscount Dundee, having ignored the advice of his officers to command his troops from a safe vantage point, had suffered the consequence of his decision to lead by example and charge into the thick of the battle. Killed by a single shot from a government musket, he lay lifeless among his fallen men.

Mackay eventually made it back to Stirling Castle, from where he made plans for his next move. The Jacobites had defeated him once, and they had proved themselves to be a formidable force under Dundee's leadership. But Dundee was dead now, and there was no one to lead the Jacobites who had Dundee's personal attributes, conviction and military skill. It is said that having heard of Dundee's death, King William remarked that it was the end of the campaign. Although the Jacobite army might not have seen his point of view, the Dutchman was to be proved right.

CHAPTER SEVEN

The Battle of Dunkeld, 21 August 1689

The Jacobite army moved into Aberdeenshire, commanded by Colonel Cannon. After news of the victory at Killiecrankie, Jacobite sympathisers were suddenly more willing to offer their support. In addition to the clansmen who had been on their way to join Dundee before the battle of Killiecrankie, more volunteers were recruited and the army grew to a considerable size. But Colonel Cannon, unfamiliar with the territory and unused to the ways of the Highlanders under his command, was hesitant about his next step. For almost a month, the newly augmented Jacobite forces moved from place to place, with government troops dogging their steps. The troops were growing increasingly restless and some of the clansmen seemed set to return home. When government troops were moved into Dunkeld, Cannon decided that the time had come to act.

The troops that had been sent to hold Dunkeld were the Cameronians, a regiment newly raised in Lanarkshire. These were not members of the Cameron clan. The Cameron clan was Jacobite. The Cameronians were formed from the ranks of the most committed of the Covenanters and the regiment was named after their leader, Richard Cameron, who had lost his life during their struggle. These men had been bitter enemies of the Stewart monarchs and of John Graham of Claverhouse, Viscount Dundee. Now they had formed themselves into a fighting force to support the new king. They numbered less than one thousand men. Their commander, Lieutenant-Colonel William Cleland, was only 28 years old, but he was no stranger to battle, having fought with the Covenanters at Bothwell Brig and Drumclog ten years previously.

The Cameronians arrived in Dunkeld on 17 August. The town was small and had no fortifications, but the men made the best use of the protection offered by the cathedral and the mansion of Dunkeld House and the enclosure around it. They made these the centre of their defences, digging trenches and erecting barricades elsewhere around the town to strengthen their position. The next few days were extremely tense. Jacobites from the surrounding district began to arrive and demanded the Cameronians' surrender. Cleland held firm, and sent a message out for reinforcements. A small group of cavalry arrived to bolster Cleland's meagre force, but it was withdrawn again after a few minor skirmishes. Meanwhile, the main body of the Jacobite army under Cannon was moving nearer.

On 21 August, Cannon and the Jacobite army arrived. There were more than three times as many Highlanders as there were in Cleland's regiment, and they surrounded the little town without difficulty. But Cleland's men were not going to give up without a fight. As the Jacobite army moved into Dunkeld, the two sides fought hand-to-hand and house-to-house in a bloody and exhausting struggle. As the hours ticked by, the Cameronians were driven into a tighter and tighter knot around Dunkeld House and the cathedral. They fought desperately with pikes and muskets. When they ran out of bullets, they stripped lead from the cathedral roof to make crude substitutes so that they could continue firing. The Jacobite army was taken aback by the ferocity with which their enemies held on to their position. As the hours passed, both sides were getting exhausted, but it seemed as if the Cameronians might be forced to give up. Then, possibly as a last act of desperation, Cleland's men armed themselves with blazing faggots and began to set fire to the houses all around Dunkeld. Many of the houses were manned by Jacobites who were using them as sniping positions. If the Cameronians found a house with Jacobites inside and a lock on the door, they turned the key, setting the building ablaze with its occupants trapped inside. Soon the whole town, with the exception of the Cameronian positions, was ablaze. The Jacobite army, confused and demoralised, retreated from the inferno. In the struggle, young Colonel Cleland had been shot and killed, but his men had pulled off an incredible victory. The Jacobite commander, Cannon, was uninjured, having 'led' his men largely from behind.

Chapter Eight

The Haughs of Cromdale, 1 May 1690

> *We were in bed, sir, every man,*
> *When the English host upon us cam'.*
> *A bloody battle then began,*
> *Upon the Haughs o' Cromdale.*
> 'The Haughs o' Cromdale' – Jacobite Song

The failure to take Dunkeld had seriously undermined the Jacobites' morale, but had not yet extinguished their hopes. Although the greater part of the army dispersed to their own lands in September, Jacobite followers still made their presence felt in the Highlands, tormenting the clan chiefs who had not come out in support of them. Nonetheless, with the onset of winter, things went relatively quiet. In spring, a new general arrived to lead the Jacobites – Thomas Buchan. Buchan joined Colonel Cannon and they set about trying to rekindle people's enthusiasm for the rebellion and recruiting another Jacobite army, but it was no easy task. After moving through Badenoch in April 1690, they proceeded to Strathspey. They were in the Spey valley with a body of around 800–1000 men, when disaster struck again.

On the night of 30 April, the Jacobites arrived at the Haughs of Cromdale, level ground to the south of the village of Cromdale on the River Spey, and made camp. The men were still sleeping when Colonel Livingstone, who had been stationed in Speyside, attacked in the early hours of the morning with a force of approximately 1300 men.

The attack took the Jacobites completely by surprise. Their camp was spread out over a wide area and apart from foot soldiers guarding the fords at the River Spey to the north of their encampment, they had made little effort to make their position secure. Approaching the river while the Jacobites slept, Livingstone's army crossed the fords and overwhelmed the guards without any difficulty. They were in the midst of the Jacobite encampment before anyone could do anything to stop them. It was a slaughter. More than 300 Jacobites were killed before they had a chance to fight back and almost a third as many were taken prisoner. The darkness and the mist fortunately provided cover for the rest as they made a hasty dash for the hills to the east. The Macdonalds of Keppoch, who had camped further down the river from the main encampment, were the only group that escaped the devastation unscathed. Buchan and Cannon also escaped, but their hopes of resuscitating the rebellion had vanished along with most of their army.

Although Jacobite activity continued in small pockets of the Highlands for some time after the disaster at Cromdale, there could be no doubt that it was the end of the rebellion. The clan chiefs would not commit their men to full-scale conflict without effective organisation and leadership and that had been lost over a year ago, with the death of Viscount Dundee. Throughout 1689, there had been hopes that James would send a large army from Ireland under the duke of Berwick to reinforce the Scots Jacobites, but events in Ireland had prevented him from doing that. James's defeat at the battle of the Boyne in July 1690 completely extinguished all hopes for help from that quarter.

General Mackay, although still hampered by lack of funds, finally managed to put his plans for fortifying Inverlochy into action. He marched a large army north to Speyside before turning west for Lochaber. His force was met at Inverlochy by ships carrying the necessary supplies for the construction of his fort. After overseeing the building, he left a garrison of more than a thousand men to man it. The Highlands were still not at peace by any means, but for the present, they had been significantly subdued. It would be 25 years before a Highland army was raised again for the Stewarts.

CHAPTER NINE

The Last Outpost

The Bass Rock, in the middle of the Forth opposite North Berwick, set the scene for a last stand of Scots Jacobites against the government of William of Orange. The fortress on the rock had been used as a place of confinement for a variety of prisoners since the 15th century, most recently for Covenanters. In 1690, a small number of Jacobite prisoners were incarcerated there. In 1691, while the governor of the fortress was away on a trip to the mainland, the prisoners managed to lock out most of their guards while they were unloading coal from a supply ship at the landing place below the fortress. The guards had no option but to leave the rock on the supply ship and soon the Bass was proclaimed a Jacobite possession. It might appear to have been a pointless exercise, but the bravery and tenacity of the men who made their stand on the Bass Rock has to be admired. Having been joined by some more supporters, they held out for more than three years, getting what provisions they could from French vessels or supporters rowing out from the shore.

The fortress on the Bass Rock was in a particularly strong position. There was only one landing place on the rock, and anyone trying to land could be easily seen from the fortress above. The Jacobites had guns and ammunition and they also had cannon to repel would-be attackers. It would have been very difficult to take them by force. Although they did try to attack the fortress by sea, government forces concentrated their efforts on cutting off routes of supply to the rock to the best of their ability. One unfortunate man, who was caught trying to take supplies out to the rock in his boat, was led onto the sands at North Berwick to be hanged by government troops in full view of the rebels. The rebels fired on the hanging party with their cannon to disperse it. Unfortunately, their action did not save the condemned man's life. The hanging party moved further along the beach, out of range of the cannon on the rock, and the execution went ahead. Eventually, a blockade of government vessels managed to mount an effective blockade, preventing any supplies from reaching the rock. In April 1694, the Jacobites were forced to surrender because of lack of food.

CHAPTER TEN

The Massacre of Glencoe,
13 February 1692

Although the rebellion that Dundee had started had run out of steam, the government of King William knew that the Jacobite clans in the Highlands still had the potential to cause them serious problems. After the battle of Dunkeld, many of the clansmen remained in arms and continued to distract government troops in Scotland, raiding the territories of landowners sympathetic to the Williamite regime. The king, preoccupied with the war against France, wanted a quick solution to the perpetual disruptions in the unruly Highlands. Most importantly, he wanted to bring peace to the region without having to resort to military conflict, which would necessitate the diversion of valuable manpower from his struggle against Louis XIV.

William consulted with his secretary of state for Scotland, Sir John Dalrymple, Master of Stair. It was agreed that a strategy of buying peace in the Highlands, through offering the rebel chiefs money in exchange for promises to loyalty to the Crown, might work. The task of negotiating a settlement with the chiefs was given by Stair to John Campbell of Glenorchy, the earl of Breadalbane. Breadalbane was furnished with the sum of £12,000. The money supplied to the chiefs was intended to allow them to buy out the claims of their feudal superiors, the most important of whom was the duke of Argyll.

Breadalbane met with the chiefs at Achallader in June 1691. Discussions were not entirely amicable and one chief, Macdonald of Glencoe, left after an acrimonious debate over the money he would receive. Breadalbane wanted to reduce Macdonald's share to compensate for the theft of cattle from Campbell territory by members of the Macdonald clan. In spite of this, a state of truce was reached. The chiefs agreed to cease hostilities while messengers were sent to France to ask James Stewart to release them from their commitment to him.

Almost immediately, rumours began to circulate about Breadalbane's trustworthiness – that he had misappropriated the money supplied to him by the government, that he was secretly working for the Jacobite cause. The king resolved not to wait to see whether Breadalbane's efforts would secure a more permanent peace. In August 1691, the government issued a proclamation ordering the chiefs to take an oath of allegiance before 1 January the following year. Those chiefs who did not comply with the terms of the proclamation would have to face serious consequences.

Secretary of State Dalrymple seemed to expect that the rebel chiefs would not submit in time. In fact, it appeared that he relished the prospect of revenge. Several weeks before the deadline had been reached, he was already planning retribution on the Highland clans, his particular intent being to make an example of the Macdonalds of Glencoe. Although Macdonald of Glengarry and his men had been particularly troublesome and Dalrymple had them also in his sights, Glengarry's position was well fortified and less accessible. The Macdonalds of Glencoe, living within easy reach of Fort William, were an easier target, particularly in winter, when escape over the mountains surrounding their glen would be difficult. Moreover, as the Macdonalds were Roman Catholics, their plight would probably arouse little sympathy.

The Jacobite chiefs, meanwhile, had been forced to wait until the last minute for the dispensation from James Stewart. When news finally reached them, they had to move very quickly to take the oath of allegiance before the deadline. In spite of the reluctance they had shown to comply with King William's demands upon them, they realised that the consequences of refusal meant placing the lives of their clansmen in danger of the harshest of retribution. Accordingly, most of them set out on the journey from their home territories to take the oath of allegiance at Inverness or Inveraray.

One of the last to leave on his journey was MacIain, chief of the Macdonalds of Glencoe. At the end of December, he set out for Fort William, arriving there on the last day of the year. On his arrival, he was informed by Colonel Hill, governor of Fort William, that he could not take the oath there. The oath had to be administered by a sheriff, the nearest being at Inveraray. MacIain begged Hill to let him take the oath at Fort William, but Hill could do no more than send him on his way to Inveraray. Hill gave MacIain a letter explaining the situation to Sir Colin Campbell of Ardkinglass, the sheriff of Argyll, and a promise that no harm would come to him before his case had been considered by the privy council.

It took MacIain three days to reach Inveraray, only to discover that Campbell of Ardkinglass was away for the New Year. When Ardkinglass returned on 5 January, he was eventually persuaded by MacIain's desperate pleas to administer the oath of allegiance. He sent MacIain's signature to Edinburgh, along with those of the other chiefs of who had taken the oath at Inveraray, and enclosed a covering letter asking the privy council to consider including MacIain on the list of those who had sworn allegiance to the king before the deadline. MacIain's case was never put before the privy council. His name was struck from the list – with the approval of Dalrymple. A letter of fire and sword was drafted against all rebel chiefs and countersigned by King William on 11 January. The letter gave its recipient, Colonel Livingstone, the option of accepting surrender from those who were prepared to submit their arms and swear allegiance to the king. But Dalrymple had no plans for leniency as far as the Macdonalds of Glencoe were concerned. In a second letter, dated 16 January and also countersigned by King William, Dalrymple made it clear that MacIain's people had been selected for individual punishment as an example to others. The letter was an order for their extermination.

A detachment of 120 men under the command of Captain Campbell of Glenlyon were sent to Glencoe to carry out the terrible commission.

Glenlyon and his men arrived in Glencoe early in February 1692 and having assured the Macdonald chief that their purpose in coming to the glen was tax-collecting, were provided with sleeping quarters and generous hospitality by the people of his clan. Such was the level of secrecy that enshrouded the mission that Campbell of Glenlyon did not know the real purpose of his stay in Glencoe until 12 February. On that day, he received orders from Fort William to butcher all members of the Macdonald clan before first light the next morning. In order to ensure that the dreadful deed was carried out with maximum impact, 400 troops would be coming from Fort William and another body of troops from Ballachulish, to cut off escape routes through the glen.

Glenlyon and his men took action at the appointed time, but the ghastly affair was not carried out as quietly and efficiently as its planners had hoped. Glenlyon's men opened their attack with guns. The sound of gunfire alerted the Macdonalds to the murderers in their midst and gave many of them time to escape. The southern passes from the glen had not been covered and the troops who were supposed to guard other exits from the glen had not yet arrived. Approximately forty Macdonalds, including MacIain, were killed, but many others were able to seek refuge in the snow-covered hills.

Although the enterprise had not been carried out as effectively as Dalrymple had hoped, its effect on public opinion was striking. While the other rebel chiefs hastened to swear allegiance to King William, the news of the event was reaching the Lowlands, where enraged Jacobite supporters were quick to see the value of the story in the propaganda war against the Dutch king.

Pamphlet after pamphlet was issued, decrying the murders and the part that the king had played in them. Many people who had shown no clear resistance previously to William's accession to the throne were turned against him. William, who cared little for events in Scotland, was slow to react. Nothing was done until 1693, when a committee was eventually appointed to investigate the whole sorry affair. William's response to the findings of the committee was far from satisfactory – he tried to ignore them. The protests continued until a second committee was appointed in 1695. The Scottish parliament responded to the findings of this committee by declaring that the events at Glencoe had been an outrage for which those responsible should be punished. However, it also strenuously denied that King William was responsible to any degree. Sir James Dalrymple was removed from office and the earl of Breadalbane was imprisoned, but neither faced a trial. The Campbells escaped unpunished. William had officially been exonerated from blame, but few of his critics and none of his enemies were convinced. Mass murder had been committed and the perpetrators had escaped justice.

To a certain extent, William got what he wanted from the affair. The Jacobite chiefs had been subdued for the time being. But although they might have pledged allegiance to King William, their feelings against him had become more entrenched. Whenever the opportunity might arise for concerted action against the government, they would as willing as ever, if not more so. As things were to turn out, William did not live to see the consequences of sowing the seeds of distrust and hatred so deeply, but, years later, his successors would reap the harvest.

CHAPTER ELEVEN

The Darien Scheme

The damage that the massacre of Glencoe did to King William's reputation in Scotland was compounded by the part that he was seen to play in the failure of the Darien Scheme some years later.

It had long been felt that the union of the crowns had damaged Scottish trade. England, unlike Scotland, had a long history of enmity against France. When Scotland and England were united under the same crown, Scottish merchants suffered the consequences, as their trading links with the French were damaged because of England's conflicts with France. England, already a far richer country, had strong trading links with Asia, Africa and the Americas, but the Scots merchants were prevented from deriving any benefit from these links. Scottish merchants were treated as aliens in England, and in the English colonies. While England grew steadily richer from foreign trade, Scotland grew poorer, her traders hampered from expansion by the English at every turn. A period of poor harvests towards the end of the 17th century further impoverished the country. Many Scots were starving and of the rest, a large proportion lived from hand-to-mouth. The government in Scotland could not afford to anything about it.

In attempt to increase the country's prosperity through overseas trade, the Scottish parliament passed an act in 1693 which gave Scots merchants permission to trade in any part of the world with which the country was not at war, tax free for 21 years. Two years later, William Paterson, the Scots founder of the Bank of England, took the lead in an enterprise that was intended use these trading privileges to increase the prosperity of Scotland's traders and of the country as a whole.

Paterson's plan was to form a Scottish East India Company, based on the model of the English East India Company which had monopolised English trade with India for almost one hundred years. The Scots company would have a monopoly of trade to Africa, America and Asia, having absolute right to all the wealth that could be derived from any of the colonies it established. The Scots parliament passed the act to establish the Company of Scotland trading to Africa and the Indies on 26 May 1695. The company was to have 21 directors, 10 of whom would be Scots. Half of capital that was to be raised, £600,000, was to be provided by Scots. In November, when the subscription lists were opened in London, investors hurried to take up the opportunity. Soon £300,000 had been raised. But opposition to the company, particularly from English traders and investors in the English East India Company, was strong and protests were made by the English parliament. The company's commissioner, the marquis of Tweedale, was dismissed from his post. Under threat of legal action against them, almost all of the English investors withdrew. The English government also hampered attempts to get investment for the company from abroad, in Germany and Holland. Undaunted, the directors of the company eventually raised £400,000, almost all from Scots investors. The size of the commitment, for a country as impoverished as Scotland, was enormous.

William Paterson proposed that the first venture of the company should be the establishment of a trading colony on the Isthmus of Darien, between North and South America. Its position, roughly equidistant from Europe, Asia and Africa, was ideal for trading, it was rich in natural resources and seemed to have fertile soil for farming. The first expedition, consisting of three Scottish ships, the *Caledonia,* the *St Andrew* and the *Unicorn,* set sail from the port of Leith on 17 July 1698, landing at Darien four months later. They named the territory New Caledonia and established a town, New Edinburgh, and a fort, Fort St Andrew.

Within weeks, it had become apparent that the expedition was doomed. The settlers were completely unprepared for the tropical climate and the settlement was surrounded by mosquito-infested swamps. Malaria and other infectious diseases soon began to take their toll and many of the twelve hundred settlers died. The leaders of the expedition quarrelled. Supplies of food began to run out and ships from English colonies would not trade with them. In June 1699, seven months after landing, they decided to abandon the settlement. By the time the three ships reached their ultimate destinations of New York and Jamaica, over 350 more people had died. A second wave of settlers arrived some weeks later to find the settlement deserted. They left Darien and sailed for the West Indies. Most of those who survived the journey eventually died from the hardships they encountered there.

News of the disaster had reached Scotland by late summer 1699, but it did not deter a third expedition from setting off. When they reached Darien, they soon found out why their predecessors had abandoned the settlement as the inhospitable conditions took their toll on their numbers. Then they found themselves facing another, equally deadly enemy.

Although the Spanish had not occupied Darien, they considered it to be Spanish territory and were unwilling to risk a foreign trading settlement there, which might interfere with their interests in South America. King William, anxious to preserve his alliance with Spain against France, gave his assurance to Spain that he would not give any support to the colony, thereby effectively sanctioning Spanish attacks on the settlement. In February 1700, Spanish ships blockaded the waters around the settlement and troops were landed to attack the Fort. The settlers were forced to capitulate and, at the beginning of April, those that had not succumbed to disease, hunger, or violence set sail for the West Indies.

The Darien scheme had cost the Scots dearly. Almost 2000 lives were lost in the enterprise, at the expense of approximately £200,000 of Scots money. For many Scots, it meant financial ruin. When news of the disaster reached Scotland, there was an outcry. People were quick to recognise that William's concern for English trading interests had hindered the enterprise from the beginning. They also saw that he had ignored the interests of the Scots in his decision to side with the king of Spain. It was clear that although William was king of both Scotland and England, the interests of England, which could profit him more, came first.

CHAPTER TWELVE

The Treaty of Union

The failure of the Darien Scheme severely damaged Scotland's relations with England and engendered deep feelings of anger and mistrust in the Scots against William III. In 1701, relations between the two countries became more strained following the Act of Succession, passed by the English parliament. As William had no heirs, the throne would pass upon his death to Anne, the Protestant younger daughter of James VII and II. None of the children to whom Anne had given birth had survived childhood, and the English parliament wanted to ensure that her successor would be a Protestant. The Act of Succession stated that the English Crown should pass upon Anne's death to the Protestant rulers of Hanover and effectively increased the powers of the English parliament by denying the monarch the right to leave the country without its permission. By the time of William's death in March 1702 after a riding accident, many people in Scotland, sensing that the English parliament was asserting itself as a dominant force, had become convinced that the union of the crowns should be ended. Anne was accepted as queen of Scotland, but, in 1703, the Scottish parliament passed three acts to reassert its independence. The Act Anent Peace and War denied the right of the ruler of Scotland to take the country to war or to make alliances with other countries without the permission of the Scottish parliament. The Wine Act gave Scottish merchants the right to continue trade with France, in spite of the conflict between France and England. The third act, the Act of Security, passed in 1704, asserted the right of the Scots to choose their own monarch.

It was now clear that there was a real danger of conflict breaking out between the two nations. The English parliament reacted swiftly to the Act of Security. In 1705, it passed the Aliens Act. This act stated that unless the Scots accepted the Hanoverian succession and entered into negotiations with the English for union between the countries, Scots would be treated as aliens in England. This was a powerful threat to the Scots as it put Scots trade with English merchants in jeopardy. It also placed members of the nobility who had lands in both Scotland and England in an impossible position. Moreover, if the Scots refused to consider a union with England, it seemed as if the English might force the issue with military action against the Scots.

The idea of a union between the two countries was still strongly opposed by a majority in the Scottish parliament. Eventually, it was agreed that 31 commissioners from each country would be selected by the queen to negotiate the terms of the treaty. In April 1706, the commissioners began working out the terms of the treaty in Whitehall. From October until November, the draft of the treaty was debated in the Scottish parliament.

Under the terms of the treaty, which was presented as 25 Articles, Scotland and England would be united under the name of Great Britain, the Hanoverian succession would be guaranteed and the two kingdoms would have one parliament. The parliament would keep the structure of the present English parliament, with two separate houses – 16 Scottish peers would be elected to sit in the House of Lords and there would be 45 Scottish members elected to the House of Commons. The Scots legal system would retain its independence. The two countries would share the same coinage and system of weights and measures. Scotland was granted the same trading privileges as England, but now became liable for a share in England's national debt, which was considerably larger than its own. In compensation for the inevitable increase in tax that this would bring to the Scots, an 'Equivalent' of £398, 085 would be paid to Scotland and Scotland was granted a number of temporary tax concessions. Additionally, investors in the ill-fated Darien Scheme were offered compensation for their losses.

From the beginning of October 1706 until the beginning of the following year, the treaty was hotly debated in the Scots parliament. The Court Party, led by the duke of Queensberry, supported the idea of a union, but its members amounted to less than half of the Scottish parliament. Opposed to them were the anti-union Country Party, led by the duke of Hamilton, the Cavalier Party, which was Jacobite in sympathy, and the Squadron Volante, or New Party. In the end, the members of the Squadron Volante opted to vote in favour of the treaty. Their votes, combined with those of the Court Party, secured a narrow majority for the union. The treaty was ratified in Scotland in early January and after a comparatively easy passage through the English parliament, the Act of Union was passed in March. Two separate acts were passed at the same time as the Act of Union, preserving Presbyterianism in Scotland and Episcopacy in England. On 25 March, the Scots parliament met for the last time.

CHAPTER THIRTEEN

The Failed Rising of 1708

Whatever parliament might have voted, there were strong feelings of opposition to the union in Scotland. In Edinburgh and Glasgow, there had been riots and while parliament debated the terms of the treaty, the tide of opinion against Queensberry, Argyll and other members of the Country Party was so high that they felt their lives were in danger. Over in France, the Jacobite court in St Germain became increasingly confident that a rising at this time might stand some chance of success. James Francis Edward, who was still a child when his father died in 1701, was now old enough to play an active part in a rising. He had already had experience of fighting in the French army. The Jacobites' feelings of confidence were reinforced by the assurances from Colonel Nathaniel Hooke, an agent who had recently returned from an intelligence-gathering mission in Scotland, that an invasion from France would be readily backed up by massive support from Scottish Jacobites. Louis XIV, for his part, indicated his willingness to support the venture with men, ships and arms. The French king's readiness to offer aid was, as before, partly motivated by self-interest. His army was engaged in warfare in the Low Countries against the Dutch and the English and was under considerable pressure. The distraction afforded by an invasion of Scotland would be welcome as it might force the British to withdraw some of their troops to return to Scotland to deal with it.

On 1 March 1708, James issued a Declaration to the People of Scotland, urging the Scots to declare their support for him and rally to his standard. The terms of the declaration offered sweeping gestures of generosity. James promised a pardon to all those who had opposed the Stewarts, providing they now demonstrated their support for the Jacobite cause. He gave his word that he would call a parliament which would repeal punishing taxes and restore Scotland's independence. He guaranteed freedom of worship and full rights for Protestants. He promised amnesty and payment of arrears of pay to all enemy soldiers who defected to his cause after he landed.

Louis XIV supplied the Pretender with approximately 6000 troops and more than 30 ships. The fleet was under the command of the Comte de Forbin, the soldiers led by the Comte de Gace. Forbin was less than enthusiastic about the project, but under Louis' orders, submitted to the leadership of James Francis Edward. Unfortunately, misfortune struck before the expedition had even set off. James was struck down by measles. He was determined that the invasion should go ahead, but was still weak and ill when he boarded his ship at Dunkirk. Then an ominous sight hove into view off the French coast. The English government, informed of the threatened invasion by their spies in France, had sent a fleet of ships under the command of Admiral Byng to try to prevent the expedition from setting sail. James would not contemplate abandoning the enterprise and ordered Forbin to proceed. The weather played a hand at this point. High winds forced the English ships further out to sea and allowed the French fleet to navigate its way out of port unimpeded. After successfully evading the English ships, the fleet sailed towards Scotland.

The journey was made difficult and hazardous by adverse weather conditions. Three ships were forced to turn back. Cramped, cold and seasick, many of the troops on board the vessels that continued towards Scotland succumbed to disease. The French fleet made for the east coast of Scotland, with the intention of landing on the shores of the Forth, from where the men could disembark and move in on the capital. The plan was that upon landing, the French troops would join up with the promised Scottish supporters, who were supposed to be waiting onshore, ready to signal their presence to the French ships when they arrived in the Forth. The fleet sailed into the Forth estuary but instead of anchoring by the southern shore, anchored off the Fife coast, close to Pittenweem. Disappointingly, signals from the French ships got no response. This was possibly because the Scots, on the southern shore, did not see the signals. But it was also possible that the promised support had not arrived.

Byng's English fleet had pursued them from France and was now dangerously close. Forbin would not contemplate staying in the Forth any longer. James pleaded in vain to be put ashore to take his chances with a small body of men. Forbin refused absolutely to comply with his wishes and abandoned the invasion plan. The fleet headed north to escape the English ships. Again, James pleaded to be put ashore. The French commander, unwilling to risk his men in such an uncertain undertaking, stood firm and the fleet sailed back to France.

If a landing had been made, it is hard to say what chance the rising would have had of succeeding. On the one hand, the Jacobite fleet was carrying a large force of men and they were well provisioned with arms. When the invasion fleet arrived off the Scottish coast, government troops were extremely thin on the ground in Scotland and with the exception of Byng's fleet, opposition was disorganised. On the other hand, it seemed clear that the Scots had not rallied to the cause as Hooke had promised they would. In fact, Hooke's intelligence-gathering expeditions to Scotland had been far from thorough. He had made contact with many men of high rank in the Lowlands who professed allegiance to the exiled king, but verbal assurances were not enough. What the Jacobites needed was the support of a strong body of fighting men. Such support was only likely to come from the Jacobite Highland clans, and Hooke had made no contact with them. If the Pretender had landed, it is certainly likely that support would have been forthcoming, but it is also likely that it would have been slow to organise and piecemeal in its assembly.

The expedition had been a total failure, but lessons could be learned from it. It was clear that in future the Jacobites would not be able to count on the commitment of the French military in Scotland, unless the French could be guaranteed that there would be a concerted effort by the Scots to rise. It was also clear that effective communication and cooperation between all parties concerned would be crucial to the success of any further attempts at rebellion. Unfortunately, neither of these lessons was properly taken to heart by the time the next uprising took place in 1715.

CHAPTER FOURTEEN

Reaction to the Union, 1708–1715

Discontent with the union in Scotland had been growing. Many people had hoped for increased trade and greater prosperity, but the economic benefits of the union for Scotland were still hard to see and equal trading rights did not stop the bitter rivalry between Scots and English merchants.

In 1708, the privy council in Scotland was abolished by parliament, infuriating prominent members of the Scots nobility who were thus deprived of political influence and financial reward. The independence of the Scottish legal system then began to be undermined, in breach of the terms of the Treaty of Union. In 1709, parliament passed a Treason Act, making Scots subject to the same harsh treason law as England. In the same year, James Greenshields, an Episcopalian clergyman who had been imprisoned for using the English prayer book, appealed to the House of Lords at Westminster to overturn the judgement made against him by the Scottish Court of Session. In 1710, the House of Lords upheld his appeal, overruling the Court of Session. In effect, the Court of Session had lost much of its power.

In 1713, in contravention of the terms of the Treaty of Union, the government moved to impose a malt tax, which would seriously damage the Scottish economy. There was a violent reaction to the proposal. A bill was brought before parliament for the abolition of the union. It was rejected by only four votes. It was clear that the union was fragile. In Scotland in particular, discontent with the union and a desire for the country to regain its independence brought more people over to the Jacobite cause.

CHAPTER FIFTEEN

The Rebellion of 1715:
Background and Beginnings

After the rebellion of 1708, Jacobite intrigues continued, but there was little action. For two years, James Francis Edward was engaged in active military service with Louis' armies. He fought at the battles of Oudenarde and Malplaquet, his bravery at Malplaquet in particular earning him the respect of both the French military and their British opponents. Louis XIV was understandably too preoccupied with fighting against Marlborough's forces to concern himself any further with the Jacobite cause during this period, but Jacobite hopes were still very much alive.

Changes were taking place in Great Britain. An election in 1710 brought the Tories back into power in parliament. Amongst the Tory members of parliament were several men with Jacobite sympathies, including the duke of Ormonde, Henry St John, Viscount Bolingbroke and Robert Harley, earl of Oxford. Oxford became lord treasurer and Bolingbroke was appointed secretary of state. They still entertained hopes that the Hanoverian succession could be prevented. Queen Anne herself was not unsympathetic to her half-brother, and the two corresponded by letter. But James's determination to adhere to the Roman Catholic faith remained a stumbling block between him and succession to the throne after Anne's death.

The Tory government was faced with further difficulties over the war with France, which was costing Great Britain dearly. In order to secure an agreement for peace, the Tories were obliged to placate Protestant Whigs by agreeing to James's exile from France. In 1713, James was compelled by the terms of the Treaty of Utrecht to leave the protection of Louis XIV. He moved his court to the duchy of Lorraine. The move hampered communication between Jacobite factions in France and Scotland and diminished hopes of French support for a rebellion.

Shortly before Anne's death, a power struggle between Oxford and Bolingbroke resulted in Oxford's dismissal as treasurer. Undoubtedly, Bolingbroke had been hoping to be appointed treasurer in Oxford's place, but the dying queen chose the Whig duke of Shrewsbury instead. When she died two days later, George of Hanover was proclaimed king and a council of Whig regents was appointed to rule the country until his arrival.

James Edward Stewart travelled to France as soon as he heard of the queen's death, hoping to get the support of the French king to make his claim for the throne, but was disappointed. The ministers of Louis XIV, firm in their resolve not to violate the terms of the Treaty of Utrecht did not make him welcome and he was forced to return to Lorraine.

In the end, George I had come to the throne with barely a whimper of protest from Jacobite sympathisers. Nonetheless, there could be no doubt that the new king was unpopular, particularly with the Tories, who now found themselves ousted from power completely. In March 1715, a general election was held and the Whigs were returned to power in parliament. The Whigs were swift to act against their opponents. A number of the leading Tories were impeached, among them Bolingbroke, who fled to France.

There was widespread unrest in England and rioting broke out in several places in protest against the new regime. Jacobites seized the opportunity to rally support for James and over the next few months, the number of Jacobite sympathisers grew.

Meanwhile, on the other side of the Channel, plans were at last under way for an organised rebellion. The original scheme involved risings on three different fronts. Rebellions in Scotland and the north of England were planned, but these were to take place principally as diversions to the main rising, which was to happen at the same time in the southwest of England. The southwest was selected as the centre of the main rebellion because access from France could be facilitated by possession of the main Channel ports. There were strong pockets of dissention in the west of England and the Jacobite leaders were confident of substantial backing for the enterprise. The Pretender would land in the southwest with men, arms and supplies from France as soon as the way had been cleared for him and he would progress from there to London.

It would become clear over the next few months that the rebellion of 1715, although potentially very dangerous, was sorely lacking in two aspects: good leadership and effective communication. The most able military leader on the side of the Jacobites was undoubtedly the duke of Berwick, who had supported James's father in Ireland. But although Berwick was highly sympathetic to the cause, he had since become a marshal of France and his first loyalty was now to the French king. He was not in a position to lead an invasion of Great Britain. Viscount Bolingbroke, although less capable than Berwick, had been another potential leader, but he had fled from England. James Butler, the duke of Ormonde, was therefore selected as the leading light in the rebellion in the southwest. After the general election, Ormonde had moved away from London to Richmond. It was intended that with support of ousted Tory army officers, he would coordinate the rising. Control of major ports was essential. Accordingly, it was planned that Bristol, Plymouth and Exeter would all be taken. While the rising was still in the planning stage, however, Ormonde remained at Richmond and in July, he got news that government troops were coming to arrest him. He abandoned his plans to go to the southwest to lead the rebellion and fled to France.

With Ormonde out of the picture, hopes for the rising began to disintegrate. Responsibility for leadership now fell upon the marquess of Lansdowne, but Ormonde had told him little of what had been planned. Lansdowne proceeded to build up an arsenal at Bath, which he intended to be the centre of the rebellion, and made plans to gain control of Bristol and Plymouth. In Oxford, where support for the Jacobite cause was also strong, the duke of Ormonde's brother Arran and some other Jacobite officers were also preparing to declare for James.

The rising in the southwest never got off the ground. The government was aware that Jacobite sympathy in the region was strong. News soon got to them that plans were afoot for organised revolt and they acted swiftly to suppress it. The Habeas Corpus Act was suspended by parliament. In September and October, government troops moved in on Bristol, Bath, and Oxford. The leaders were arrested and their followers dispersed. Further arrests were made in London, Devon, and Cornwall. By the end of October, all signs of imminent rebellion had been crushed.

Events in Scotland, meanwhile, were taking shape in a different way.

CHAPTER SIXTEEN

The Rising in Scotland: Mar Takes the Initiative

> *Hey for Sandy Don!*
> *Hey for Cockolorum!*
> *Hey for Bobbing John,*
> *And his Highland quorum!*
> *Mony a sword and lance*
> *Swings at Highland hurdie;*
> *How they'll skip and dance*
> *O'er the bum o' Geordie!*
> 'Cam Ye O'er Frae France' – Jacobite song

The rising in the Scottish Highlands, planned very much as a subsidiary to the rising in England, had taken on a whole different complexion, owing to the actions of one man: John Erskine, earl of Mar. Mar was nicknamed 'Bobbing John'. It is not clear whether he was so called because of the nervous habit he had of twitching his head or because of his ability to change his allegiance whenever the occasion demanded it. Mar had been an active politician for many years, serving in government during the reigns of William and Mary and of Anne. He had played a leading role in the negotiations around the Treaty of Union and had helped to push it through the Scottish parliament. From 1713, he had held the position of secretary of state for Scotland. Although Mar was a Tory, he had voiced no opposition to the accession of George I and, when the Hanoverian king came to the throne in 1714, he had written a letter to him, offering to serve him in government. Mar's overtures were ignored and the king did not give him a position in the new government.

At the beginning of August the following year, Mar was insulted further when the king turned his back on him in public and refused to speak to him. Mar's response was swift. He left London at once and travelled north in disguise on a coal ship from Gravesend, bound for Newcastle, accompanied by General George Hamilton and a handful of servants. From Newcastle, the party sailed on another vessel to the East Neuk of Fife. As soon as he landed in Scotland, Mar made contact with Jacobite sympathisers and arranged for word to be spread that he was assembling an army on behalf of the Pretender. He travelled first to Kinnoull, in Perthshire, where he spent a few days with Thomas Hay, earl of Kinnoull. Thomas Hay's son, Colonel John Hay, joined up with Mar. Mar then travelled north to his own estates on Deeside where he organised a *tinchal,* a great hunt, inviting all the prominent leaders from whom he hoped to gain support.

Although Mar's move to Scotland appears to have been a spur-of-the-moment decision, he had probably been playing a careful game for some time, keeping the lines of communication open with the Jacobite court in St Germain at the same time as he was seeking the favour of George I. Mar was no great military leader, as the forthcoming campaign would show. But he was an ambitious politician and had probably been waiting to see which side offered him the better chance of political advancement.

In the early stages of his campaign, many people were uncertain whether or not Mar was acting with the explicit consent of the Pretender. Sensing unease amongst some of his potential supporters because of this, the bold earl bluffed, producing a document which he claimed was a commission from James. The first document he produced was probably a fake: he did not have a proper commission from the Pretender until he received one dated 7 September, by which time the rebellion was already under way.

Where bluffing failed him, Mar bullied. Amongst those who expressed reluctance to join Mar without proof of a commission from James was John Farquharson of Invercauld, one of Mar's vassals. Farquharson decided that the loyalty he owed to Mar as his feudal superior was not enough to make him follow him if he was acting without the king's express authority. Farquharson baled out, leaving his home at Invercauld on the night that Mar came to stay with him. Mar, enraged, vented his wrath on Farquharson's tenants. On Mar's estates at Kildrummy, there was obvious reluctance amongst many of the tenants to come out in support of the rebellion. A threatening letter to his baillie, Jock Forbes, brought the hesitating tenants into line.

The hunting party organised by Mar saw a great many prominent nobles gathering at Braemar. Mar delivered an address at the meeting. He expressed his sincere regret for the part he had played in bringing about the union of the parliaments. He emphasised his contempt for George I, the oppressor. He spoke of the promise of James Stewart to liberate the country on his return to the throne and described, in enthusiastic terms, the massive support that the risings in both Scotland and England would get, from at home and from France. By the end of the meeting, he had pledges of backing from most of those present.

A second meeting was held at Aboyne on 3 September at which the leaders were told to call their men to arms. On 21 August, Louis XIV had died. The news of the French king's death made some of the Jacobite leaders hesitate. They felt that it would be better to wait for assurances from James that the regency of the young Louis XV would be willing to back the rebellion before continuing. But the general consensus of opinion was that it was too late to abandon their plans and that the rising should go ahead. On 6 September, the Stewart standard was raised at Braemar. Some days later, Mar moved from Braemar to Kirkmichael. By this time, Mar had an army of several hundred, which was reinforced in the coming days by troops from Atholl under the command of the marquis of Tullibardine, Lord Drummond and his cavalry and others. Mar kept up the campaign to rally Jacobite sympathisers by sending letters and manifestos out all over Scotland calling upon the services of all those loyal to the Jacobite cause.

Colonel John Hay, one of the first men to join Mar, played an active role in the early days of the rebellion. On 14 September, Hay's men took control of Perth, with the help of Jacobite sympathisers in the town, who provided boats for Hay's men to cross the Tay. The town had prepared to defend itself with a force of men sent by the duke of Atholl, but when Hay's troops arrived at the city, the duke's men, far from resisting, joined them. Although the duke of Atholl had not agreed to join the rising, his sons, the marquis of Tullibardine, Lord George Murray and Lord Charles Murray, had all taken the side of the Jacobites. It was now clear that the duke's men agreed with his sons' decision. Mar appointed Hay governor of Perth and sent in reinforcements before moving into the town himself on 28 September, accompanied by a growing force of Highlanders.

Although Mar's army was low in funds and supplies, his confidence was high. He had assurances that money and supplies would be coming from France and that James Francis Edward would also be landing in the country soon. Perth was secure, and to the north and east, the country was more or less under Jacobite control. The Jacobite army now numbered well over 10,000 men.

CHAPTER SEVENTEEN

The Rallying of the Western Clans

The west of the country was still not secure. Although Mar had had promises of support from the western clans, this did not materialise in the initial stages of the rising. At Inveraray, the duke of Argyll's brother, Archibald Campbell, earl of Islay, posed a possible threat to the Jacobite cause and was rallying support. Inveraray was being fortified with heavy defences and Campbell had gathered a force of more than a thousand men.

In mid-September, Mar sent General George Gordon of Achintoul to organise support for the Jacobites from the clans in the west and to capture Inveraray.

Gordon met up with Alexander Macdonald of Glengarry and Grant of Genmoriston at the Braes of Glenorchy in late September. Reinforcements were slow in coming, but by the end of the first week of October they had been joined by a body of Macdonalds of Clanranald, and around three hundred of the notorious MacGregor clan. The total number of Jacobites assembled under Gordon now amounted to approximately 1300 men. They now moved to Inveraray, but finding it heavily fortified and well manned, did not attack the town. A week was spent encamped a short distance from the town and although a few minor skirmishes took place, no decisive action was taken. Further reinforcements had swelled the numbers of Jacobites to around 1900 men. They might have made an assault on Inveraray. They might have moved south and attacked Glasgow, or east, to tackle Argyll's force at Stirling, but in the event, they took no action. Towards the end of October, they were ordered by Mar to leave Inveraray and join up with his forces in Perthshire.

CHAPTER EIGHTEEN

The Raid on Edinburgh Castle

While Mar was occupied assembling his army and moving into Perth, Jacobites in Edinburgh had also been taking action. Their plan, to capture the castle, was daring to say the least, for Edinburgh was strongly pro-government. Had they succeeded, they would have made a valuable contribution to the rising. If the castle had been captured, it would have been easier for Jacobite troops to move in on the capital. Control of Edinburgh would have made communication with Jacobite forces to the south much easier. The castle garrison was poorly provisioned with food and clothing, but there were arms inside, and ammunition and money, which would have proved very useful. It is not known whether or not Mar was made aware of the plans that were being made, although his position would have been much improved, had it succeeded.

The figure at the head of the scheme was a man called Thomas Arthur, formerly a soldier in the regular army. To support him, he had a group of Jacobite sympathisers from the town along with Lord Drummond, son of the duke of Perth and 50 of his men.

The plan was simple in design and should have been simple in execution. It might well have succeeded had it not been for careless talk and poor timekeeping. Thomas Arthur had identified three members of the garrison in the castle, two sentries and a sergeant, who were willing to help the attackers in return for financial reward. On the appointed night, at the appointed time, these men were to let down ropes from the castle battlements to the Jacobites, who would be waiting below with rope ladders. Once the ladders had been tied to the ropes, the soldiers in the castle would pull them up and fasten them to the top of the battlements. The attackers would climb up and take the sleeping garrison by surprise. The rope ladders for scaling the wall were to be made and brought to the site on the night by a man called Charles Forbes.

It was Arthur, architect of the plan, who made the first mistake. Rather than seeing the sense of keeping the whole affair strictly between conspirators, he told his brother what was going to happen. His brother, a doctor, confided in his wife. The good doctor's wife, unfortunately, was not sympathetic to the Jacobite cause. As soon as she heard of the proposed assault on the castle, she passed on the news anonymously to Sir Adam Cockburn of Ormiston, the lord justice clerk.

It was a matter of only an hour or so before the attack was about to happen when Cockburn was told of the plans. He arranged for extra patrols of the town guard to be made around the foot of the castle rock and sent a message to the garrison giving warning of the plot. The governor of the castle was not in residence that night. When the deputy governor, Lieutenant-Colonel Stewart, received the news of the threatened attack, his reaction was surprisingly casual. Whether he dismissed the news as unsubstantiated rumour or simply felt that the castle was impregnable, he did not take the threat seriously. He increased the number of sentries on patrol before he retired for the night, but beyond that, did nothing.

Stewart's reaction had much in common with that of the owner and customers of a tavern in the town where some of the conspirators met that night to fortify themselves with a drink before their exploit. The conspirators, their tongues no doubt loosened by alcohol, were far from discreet. By the time they had left the tavern, their secret was known to a number of people. Nevertheless, nothing was done. In spite of Arthur's blunder and the other conspirators' careless talk, the attack still had a reasonable chance of succeeding at this point if everyone played their part as planned.

The Jacobite attackers gathered at the foot of the castle rock at 11 p.m. on the northwest side. Their allies in the castle above gave the signal that all was ready and let down the ropes. Unfortunately, the attackers were not as ready as the soldiers. Charles Forbes had not yet arrived with the ladders. The men in the castle grew impatient. Time was of the essence if they were to avoid being caught by the sentries on patrol. The attackers had a number of ladders with them and decided to go ahead with what they had got. They tied them to the ropes and the men above hauled them up. When the ladders had been attached to the battlements, however, the attackers realised that they were too short. The ladders dangled several feet above the ground, hopelessly out of reach.

There was no time to look for a solution to the dilemma. As the Jacobites stood at the foot of the castle rock, wondering what to do next, the men above signalled to them that the sentry patrol in the castle was approaching. Anxious to conceal the truth about what had been happening from the approaching guards, the men in the castle then detached the ropes from the battlements, threw them down the rock, took out their guns and began firing upon the men below. The men at the foot of the rock scattered, one of them falling and injuring himself in the process. The noise and confusion alerted a patrol of the town guard, who then gave chase as the Jacobites beat a hasty retreat to the far side of the Nor' Loch. Charles Forbes, now more than thirty minutes late for the rendezvous, was just making his way towards the castle with the ladders when he met the party hurrying in the opposite direction.

Four of the attackers were caught, but were lucky enough to escape without punishment, as there was no substantial evidence against them. The men in the castle were much less fortunate. The two privates, James Thomason and Thomas Holland, were flogged for their part in the conspiracy. The sergeant, a man called William Ainslie, was tried and condemned to death. After his execution, his body hung from the battlements of Edinburgh Castle for two weeks. The deputy governor of the castle was dismissed from his post and imprisoned in the Tolbooth.

CHAPTER NINETEEN

Argyll Moves North

From the earliest stages of Mar's campaign, the government had become painfully aware of the threat that they faced in Scotland. Glasgow, a Whig stronghold, was secure, as was much of the south-west of Scotland. Edinburgh was also pro-government. But should Mar proceed with a policy of active aggression, there were precious few government troops in Scotland to act against him as most of the regular army had been disbanded after the end of the wars with France. Troops from England could not be spared because of the rising in the southwest. Apart from a contingent of troops at Stirling and a small force hastily assembled in the capital, the government had little with which to retaliate.

Shortly after the Stewart standard was raised at Braemar, John, duke of Argyll, was appointed to take command of the government forces in Scotland and travelled north from London. He was an able military leader, but the size of the force that had so far been mustered on the king's behalf was dwarfed by the number of Jacobites under Mar's command. Argyll went to Edinburgh first, where, on 14 September, he made an inspection of the garrison at the castle and appointed a new deputy governor, Alexander Grant of Grant, to replace the disgraced James Stewart. From Edinburgh, he moved to Stirling, where the numbers of the force under his command were increased by three battalions of volunteers from Glasgow. He now had an army of over 2000, but they were not all trained men. His position was precarious and he was well aware of it.

CHAPTER TWENTY

The Expedition to Burntisland

Mar's position was strong and still getting stronger. While the bulk of Mar's army remained in Perth, a small excursion led by the master of Sinclair did much to boost morale for the Jacobite forces. Early one morning at the beginning of October, the master of Sinclair received news that a ship carrying a cargo of weapons and ammunition was lying in the harbour at Burntisland. The guns and ammunition were being transported north, for the troops of the earl of Sutherland, a government supporter. The ship would only be staying in harbour until late high tide, which would be at around midnight. Sinclair consulted with Mar and got his permission to take an expedition with Major Harry Balfour to capture the cargo. The expedition was not without its difficulties: the unruly Highlanders who accompanied the horsemen and baggage horses proved difficult to control and took the opportunity of being freed from the confines of Perth to plunder wherever the opportunity presented itself, drink whatever they could find and generally misbehave. In spite of this, the ship was captured and its cargo was unloaded and brought back to Perth. The mission had been accomplished in 24 hours, which was a considerable achievement.

CHAPTER TWENTY-ONE

Mackintosh of Borlum Crosses the Forth

In the first week of October, Mar was joined by the Mackintosh clan, under the command of Mackintosh of Borlum. With Borlum was his nephew, Lieutenant-Colonel Mackintosh. The marquis of Huntly brought more than 2000 troops, including 500 horse, to join the army in Perth. Earl Marischal and James Keith Marischal, the earl's brother, also arrived with a body of several hundred troops. In the north of Scotland, the earl of Seaforth had raised a force of around 4000 for the Jacobite cause.

The rebellion was spreading. In early October, just after Mackintosh of Borlum arrived in Perth, Mar received word of a rising of Jacobites in Northumberland, and a request for help. Another rising was planned in the Scottish Borders, in Dumfries and Galloway. All this was happening concurrently with the gathering of the clans in the west. The total number of fighting men who were now at Mar's disposal in Perth, in the north and in the west, now amounted to more then 12,000 – and may have totalled as much as 16,000. Mar's position was extremely strong. Had he used the resources at his command to take decisive and concerted action at this point, he could very likely have defeated Argyll, captured Stirling and Edinburgh and had the whole of Scotland under his control.

But this was not to happen. The reason why Mar hesitated has long been a matter of conjecture. The clans from the west had not yet joined with the main body at Perth, nor had Seaforth's men, who would swell the size of the Jacobite army considerably. In all probability, Mar wanted to wait for their arrival before he made his move. In addition to this, Mar may have been relatively rich in human resources, but he was severely financially restricted. He had managed to raise money whilst in Perth through collection of cess (tax), but he was also was anxious for promised money and supplies to arrive from abroad. Lastly, he still remained hopeful that the Pretender would be arriving in Scotland and along with him, a force of French soldiers under the command of Berwick. In Mar's mind, these may have been the key to ultimate success. But time was running out for him. Whether he knew it or not, the rebellion in the southwest of England had been extinguished. Now that the threat to London had been swept aside, the government was free to turn their attentions and their troops northwards.

On 9 October, Mar finally made a move, but it seems that he was still holding back from committing himself to a final plan. Mackintosh of Borlum was sent out from Perth with 2000 men, en route for the East Neuk of Fife, from where they would cross the Forth and move south to join up with the English Jacobites in Northumberland.

The decision to split his force in this way might have appeared risky, but if it had been followed through according to a clear plan, could have produced significant benefits for the Jacobites. With Argyll in Stirling guarding the river fords there, the crossing of the Forth was the biggest obstacle between the Jacobites in the north and those in the south. Once a crossing had been achieved, a concerted effort between the two forces could have brought Argyll to his knees. If Mackintosh managed to gather the Border Jacobites and Northumbrian Jacobites together, there was a possibility that an attack could then be launched simultaneously, by Mar from Perth and Mackintosh from the south, on Argyll's army in Stirling.

Unfortunately, it seems that Borlum's instructions were unclear from the beginning. After initial success, Borlum's expedition turned into what was at best, a diversion and at worst, a fiasco.

Borlum led his men to the northern shores of the Forth in East Fife. A body of around 500 men was sent to Burntisland to distract government ships in the Firth of Forth from the main centre of operations. Fishing boats were organised from all the ports along the East Fife coast to ferry Mackintosh's men across to the southern shores, in East Lothian. The crossing was a remarkable achievement. The whole operation was conducted in the hours of darkness and lasted two nights. On the second night, things did not go quite so smoothly. One of the Jacobite ships, carrying approximately 40 men, was captured. Some others, in their efforts to evade government vessels, were forced back and landed on the Isle of May in the middle of the Forth. They eventually escaped from there and travelled back to Perth some days later. In spite of these difficulties, over 1500 men were successfully landed in East Lothian and were gathered in Haddington on 14 October.

Mackintosh's next move took many by surprise. Instead of marching on from Haddington towards the Borders, he turned back with his men towards Edinburgh. Rather than launching an assault on the capital itself, he moved in on the port of Leith. The 40 prisoners taken from the captured ship were freed from imprisonment in the tolbooth and ships in the harbour were raided for arms. The customs house provided the Jacobites with ample supplies of food and drink. Armed with their booty, Mackintosh's men then barricaded themselves in the Citadel, with whatever makeshift defences they could find.

News of Mackintosh's crossing of the Forth had already reached Argyll, who had set off from Stirling with a body of troops and headed for Edinburgh with all speed. He arrived at Edinburgh the day after Mackintosh and headed towards Leith. Seeing that the Jacobites were in a relatively secure position, Argyll decided not to waste valuable time and manpower laying siege to the Citadel. He had around 500 men with him, and their absence from Stirling meant that the government troops there were in a much weaker position and at great risk if Mar should attempt an attack from Perth at this point. It was unlikely that Mackintosh would make an assault on Edinburgh, for the element of surprise was lost and the capital had had time to make defensive preparations. In these circumstances, discretion was the better part of valour. Consequently, Argyll withdrew to Edinburgh. That night, Mackintosh led his men quietly out of the Citadel and down the coast. They moved less than ten miles, to Seaton House in East Lothian, and after gathering plentiful supplies of food from the neighbourhood and digging entrenchments, they set up an encampment there.

Argyll, who was still in Edinburgh, was preparing to attack Seaton House when he heard that Mar had left Perth and was moving towards Stirling. Leaving a detachment of 250 men to help defend the capital, he marched the rest of his force back to Stirling at speed. Mar, it seems, thought better of a confrontation. He only got as far as Dunblane before turning back to Perth.

Mackintosh of Borlum stayed in Seaton House until 19 October, when he left for the Borders.

CHAPTER TWENTY-TWO

The Rebels in Northumberland

In England, following the threatened rebellion in the southwest, the government had been at great pains to extinguish all other likely sources of further resistance. One measure that was taken was to order the arrest of leading Jacobites all over the country. It is thought that it was largely as a result of this measure that the rebellion in Northumberland began. At the head of the rebellion was Thomas Forster, MP for Northumberland. He responded to the news of his imminent arrest by organising a meeting of Jacobites in Northumberland. He joined forces with James Radcliffe, earl of Derwentwater, and then with Thomas Errington, from Beaufront Castle near Corbridge. They were a small band of around 150 horsemen – not a trained fighting force, but a collection of Northumbrian landowners, tenants and servants. Although most of the force was composed of Roman Catholics, Forster, a Protestant, was elected as leader as it was thought that Protestant leadership would make people more forthcoming in their support for the rising.

The gathering moved to Rothbury, from where Forster wrote to Mar asking for reinforcements and supplies. Then they travelled east, to the town of Warkworth, close to the coast. They arrived in Warkworth on 7 October, where King James III was proclaimed and their numbers were increased by a number of Jacobite horsemen who had rallied at Coldstream. Forster's little company stayed a few days in Warkworth. The professed object of the rising was an advance on Newcastle, but time was passing, and in Newcastle, the Whigs were already preparing defence of the town.

While Forster lingered in Warkworth, Lindisfarne Castle on Holy Island was taken for the Jacobites in a daring enterprise by a man called Lancelot Errington. Errington was in command of a merchant vessel that had been supplying the small garrison at Lindisfarne Castle on the island with provisions. When he landed with provisions on 10 October, most of the soldiers from the garrison came to help with the unloading. Errington invited them to board his ship for a drink. Having made sure that they had enjoyed his hospitality to the point of complete inebriation, Errington found that their capture was a relatively simple matter. He overpowered the rest of the guards and took possession of the castle. Holy Island was a potentially valuable asset. If French ships were coming as expected to support the rising, possession of the island would have facilitated communication with the approaching vessels. Unfortunately, Errington held the island for only one day. Before reinforcements could get to him, he was overwhelmed by a company of soldiers sent by the governor of Berwick Castle and taken prisoner.

Forster's force, which had doubled in size, eventually moved north from Warkworth to Alnwick. From Alnwick, they moved to Hexham, and while the dwindling possibility of an attack on Newcastle was still being debated, Forster received news that Jacobites from the southwest of Scotland had arrived at Rothbury. By this time aware that Newcastle was now under the command of General Carpenter who was bringing in troops to fortify the town, so Forster readily abandoned his hesitant advance and turned north instead, to meet up with the Scots.

CHAPTER TWENTY-THREE

The Rebels in the Southwest of Scotland

The southwest of Scotland was largely dominated by Whig supporters, but nonetheless, in Dumfries and Galloway there were
pockets of support for the Jacobite cause, with a number of the local
gentry being involved, including William Gordon, Viscount
Kenmuir, William Maxwell, earl of Nithsdale and Robert Dalziel,
earl of Carnwath. Forced to decide between declaring loyalty to the
government of George I and becoming rebels, these three men, led
by Kenmuir, chose the latter option and made preparations for
action at the beginning of October. After assembling at Moffat, with
a force of less than 200 horsemen between them, their first aim was
to take Dumfries. They moved towards Dumfries on 12 October,
but realising that the Whigs in the town, under the command of the
marquis of Annandale, were being mobilised against them, they
changed course and headed for Lochmaben. From there they proceeded to Ecclefechan, where they were joined by Sir William
Maxwell of Springkell and a few more horsemen. It was now 14
October. The modest force, which had not increased significantly
in numbers, moved on, first to Langholm and then to Hawick. An
advance on Kelso was halted when it became clear that there was a
danger of substantial resistance there. They had spent several days,
almost constantly on the move, and there had still been no substan-
tive action.

On 17 October, news came to them from General Forster that
they should meet up with the English Jacobites. After proclaiming
James III in Jedburgh on 18 October, they marched on to Rothbury,
where they were joined by the company under Forster on

19 October. After a night's rest and recuperation, the two forces moved on, to Wooler. While they were resting at Wooler they received intelligence that Mackintosh of Borlum had reached Duns with his force of Highlanders and accordingly, they continued moving north to meet up with Mackintosh at Kelso. The threatened resistance at Kelso had melted away in the face of the two-pronged advance. The Jacobites moved in, Mackintosh from the west and Forster and Kenmuir from south, without any opposition. On 24 October, two days after their arrival, James III was proclaimed king in the centre of the town.

CHAPTER TWENTY-FOUR

Mackintosh, Kenmuir, and Forster

The force led by Mackintosh of Borlum was smaller than it had been when he set out from Perth, but still numbered around 1400 foot. The cavalry of the combined Northumbrian and Border contingents amounted to around 600. The three forces together therefore made quite a sizeable army. Unfortunately, it lacked cohesion and strong, unified leadership, and most importantly of all, it lacked a clear objective. Had Mar issued explicit instructions to the leaders at any point – better still, had he assigned overall leadership to one man at any point – the army of Kenmuir, Forster, and Borlum might have helped him to take the whole of Scotland for the king. But Mar had no real command of the situation – nor did it seem that he wished to take real responsibility for it. Although he had been in contact with Mackintosh, Forster, and Kenmuir separately and seemed keen for them to join forces, he left the decision for what was to happen next – whether it be an advance into England or a move north to Stirling – up to them. After his tentative advance towards Stirling while Argyll was in Edinburgh, Mar was not prepared to make another move until he had been joined by the western clans under General Gordon and Lord Seaforth's men from the north.

Left thus to their own devices, the leaders debated what to do next. And while the Jacobites wasted time in Kelso, unable to reach an agreement, General Carpenter mobilised a force of 1000 men from Newcastle and began marching north towards them.

The Jacobites had three options. The first one was to prepare to face Carpenter and his army. They had every possibility of success and a victory would boost morale among Jacobite supporters and possibly encourage others to commit to the cause. The second option was to leave Kelso and make a move to the west, taking decisive action to capture Whig strongholds in the southwest of Scotland for James before moving on to Glasgow. Once Glasgow had been taken, an assault on Stirling with the help of Mar's army from Perth would bring the government to its knees in Scotland. The third choice, supported vigorously by Forster and the Northumbrians, was to march west to Carlisle then south into Lancashire. There were a great many Jacobites in Lancashire and it was hoped that the arrival of a Jacobite force would bring them out en masse to support the rebellion.

Kenmuir and Forster were united in their opposition to the first option, which had been strongly supported by Borlum. Neither relished the thought of a confrontation with Carpenter. Both had already shown that they were not really prepared to commit to aggressive action. Kenmuir had avoided battle at Dumfries and Kelso. Forster had been glad to turn back from his advance on Newcastle. The second option was fiercely opposed by the English Jacobites, who didn't want to go into Scotland and the third, by the Scots, who didn't want to venture south of the border.

A compromise of indecision eventually led the army out of Kelso to Jedburgh, Hawick, and Langholm. Travelling along the border, they were still unsure of their ultimate destination. From Langholm, scouts were sent out to investigate the possibility of taking Dumfries and returned with the news that it was well defended. As far as the English contingent was concerned, this settled the matter. If Dumfries could not be taken, they should march into England. They had generous offers of support from the Lancashire Jacobites – thousands of men, it was claimed, were ready to rise at a moment's notice. The Scots contingent was divided. Refusing to cross the border, some 500 of Mackintosh's men departed and headed back towards Perth. The remainder reluctantly stayed with the main force and headed south with Forster's army.

The army marched into Cumberland and reached Penrith on 2 November, encountering very little opposition en route except a half-hearted attempt to resist their advance by the Westmoreland militia. From Penrith, they progressed via Kendal and Lancaster, where King James was proclaimed, on to Preston. The journey took several days and was made difficult by harsh weather conditions, but the army encountered no significant resistance en route. The horse reached Preston a day before the infantry, which arrived on 10 November. Their numbers, depleted by the departure of so many of the Highlanders at Langholm and by a few more desertions since then, were increased by around 1500 men when they reached Preston. After resting his men for a day or two, Forster intended pressing on to Manchester, where he anticipated that they would be joined by a great many more supporters. Unfortunately, he soon discovered that the government forces were closing in and the possibility of an advance on Manchester had already been ruled out. An army led by General Wills had come north from Cheshire and was already north of Manchester and heading towards Preston. A second force, led by Carpenter, was approaching from the east.

The Jacobite force barricaded themselves in Preston while the government armies closed in on them. Rather than taking up a defensive position at the crossing of the River Ribble, to the south of the town, the Jacobites made the decision to set up their defences round the centre of the town. The decision made sense in one respect. Having a smaller area to defend, their troops would not be spread too thinly and all routes into the centre could be adequately covered. On the other hand, if they had set up a line of defence at the Ribble, they might have been able to prevent the government troops from completely surrounding them, which is what happened.

Wills' force arrived first, on 12 November. His first attack on the town was successfully repulsed after fierce fighting, in which more than a hundred government soldiers lost their lives. Comparatively few Jacobites were killed. In spite of Wills' forces making repeated

attempts to storm the barricades from all directions, the Jacobites
still held the centre of the town. The fighting died out during the
night and all was quiet apart from occasional bursts of sniper fire.
Although Wills had deployed his men carefully around the town,
he had left a route to the southwest of the town unguarded. A large
number of the Jacobite troops decided to slip away under cover of
darkness while they still had the opportunity for escape and took
this route, across the Penwortham ford. Next morning, General
Carpenter arrived with more than 2000 men to bolster the government forces. Carpenter wasted no time in taking command of the
situation and blocking all possible routes out of Preston. Within a
couple of hours of his arrival, the Jacobites realised that there was
now no question of escape. Forced with the choice between surrender and attempting to fight their way out of the predicament, the
Jacobites were split in two. Forster and the English Jacobites were
all for surrender and Forster began at once to try to negotiate for
favourable terms. The Highlanders saw no honour in this and were
in favour of fighting to the last. Wills agreed to give the Jacobites
time to consider their position in exchange for hostages. Lord
Derwentwater and Colonel Mackintosh surrendered themselves as
hostages overnight while the matter was debated. The next morning, Wills got what he wanted. Feeling betrayed by Forster, the
Scots reluctantly had decided to capitulate. The government troops
moved in to accept their surrender and take possession of their
weapons.

It was a humiliating and painful surrender and the prisoners were
treated harshly. Some officers who were identified as having
defected from the regular army were court-martialled and put to
death there and then. The Jacobites of low rank were herded into
the church at Preston and were kept there in cold, squalid conditions for a month before being accommodated in other prisons. Few
escaped. Some were deported and some died in prison. Thirty were
executed. Other officers and the leaders of the rising were taken to
London for trial. Derwentwater and Kenmuir were beheaded.
Winton, Forster, Derwentwater's brother, Charles Radcliffe, and

Mackintosh of Borlum all managed to escape from Newgate prison before their trials, as did a number of others.

While the Jacobites in Preston were suffering the humiliation of defeat, their comrades in Scotland were preparing for battle at Sheriffmuir.

CHAPTER TWENTY-FIVE

Preparations for Action: a Small Victory for Argyll

Since Borlum had made his daring crossing of the Forth, little had been achieved by Mar in Perth. His tentative advance towards Stirling while Argyll was otherwise occupied in Edinburgh had lacked conviction and was too late. After retreating back to Perth he spent most of his time trying to raise money to support his impoverished army while waiting to be joined by General Gordon and the western clans and from the north, the earl of Seaforth and his men. Mar's money-raising strategy was a combination of straight demands for money from merchants, landowners and towns and the raising of cess on valued rent – 20 shillings for every 100 pounds (Scots) of rent value.

In late October, Major Graham and Colonel Gordon of Glenbucket were sent with around 300 foot and 80 cavalry to Dunfermline, to collect taxes on behalf of Mar. As a gesture of defiance, Graham's men did not take the direct route from Perth to Dunfermline but instead took a slight detour, passing close to Castle Campbell at the head of Dollar Glen, which was manned by a small garrison of Argyll's men. It was a rash move, drawing the attention of the government forces to their presence in the area. The party reached Dunfermline on the night of 23 October and the officers refreshed themselves in taverns around the town before settling down for a good night's sleep. They gave little thought to matters of security or to how they might rally and defend themselves should the need arise. A solitary sentry was placed on the road into the town from Stirling. Another was posted outside the abbey, where most of the Highland soldiers were sleeping.

Argyll had been quick to react to the Jacobites' detour past Castle Campbell. Lieutenant-Colonel Charles Cathcart had been sent in pursuit of them with 200 dragoons and while the Jacobites slept, he planned an unpleasant surprise. Having determined that the main body of soldiers was in the abbey, he sent his men into the town at five o'clock in the morning. After killing the sentry guarding the road into the town, the government troops carried out a swift and effective surprise attack on the Jacobite officers. They captured 18 men then retreated in haste before the Highlanders in the abbey could be roused and organised to retaliate. It was a humiliating episode for the Jacobites, especially Graham and Glenbucket, and it did much to boost the morale of the government troops.

Back in Perth, Mar was aware that he had to take decisive action at some point soon. As October drew to a close, it became clear that he could delay no longer. The clans from the west under General Gordon, around 2500 men in total, were now on the way to join the main force. The earl of Seaforth was approaching from the north with another 3000 men. The Jacobite army was about to reach its ultimate strength. Meanwhile, Argyll's force, which at present amounted to a quarter of the size of Mar's, was about to be rein-forced significantly. Three regiments of infantry were arriving from Ireland and 6000 troops from Holland were about to be brought over to join him. It was imperative that action was taken before Argyll's army increased any further.

CHAPTER TWENTY-SIX

From Perth to Sheriffmuir

Will ye go tae Sheriffmuir,
Bauld John o' Innisture,
There tae see the noble Mar
And his Hieland laddies.
A' the true men o' the north,
Angus, Huntly and Seaforth,
Scouring on tae cross the Forth
Wi' their white cockadies.
        'Will Ye Go Tae Sheriffmuir?' – Jacobite song

On 9 November, once Seaforth had arrived in Perth, a council of war was held and plans were made for the move south. The main objective of the plan was to make a successful crossing of the Forth before moving on, via Edinburgh, to the border and across into England. The crossing of the Forth was to be made by the main force at a ford above Stirling, while a diversionary force of around 3000 men was to be used to launch a three-pronged attack on Argyll's army in Stirling. One body of men was to attack the causeway leading up to the bridge at Stirling, a second was to make an assault at the ford at Cambuskenneth Abbey, approximately a mile down the river and a third was to move in upstream from the town, at the Dripcobble.

On 10 November, Mar's army marched out of Perth and met up with General Gordon's men at Auchterarder, 13 miles to the southwest. Three battalions were left in Perth under the command of Major Balfour to guard the town. Meanwhile, Argyll, having been informed by spies from Perth of every detail of Mar's plan, was preparing to move out of Stirling and travel north to prevent the Jacobite army from reaching the River Forth. He called in the three regiments from Ireland that had arrived in Glasgow and summoned back General Wightman and the men he had left in Edinburgh. On 12 November, he led his army out of Stirling.

At Auchterarder, the Jacobite army spent two nights. On 11 November, Mar carried out a review of his troops. On 12 November, the army moved on. General Gordon's men were sent in front to capture Dunblane, to the north of Stirling, before the main force reached it. By afternoon, Gordon was approaching Kinbuck, to the north of Dunblane, when a messenger came with the news that Argyll's army had marched from Stirling, and north through Dunblane. Darkness was falling. It would be unsafe to continue much further, with the risk of coming across Argyll's army in the dark. Gordon's men kept moving until they reached Kinbuck, where they set up camp for the night. The rest of the Jacobite army joined them there, Mar both surprised and angry that his plans to take Dunblane had been thwarted. Just over two miles away, on high ground a short distance to the northeast of Dunblane, Argyll's army was arranged in battle formation, waiting for morning.

At six in the morning, the Jacobite army was formed into battle order, just to the east of the village of Kinbuck. After almost two hours of waiting in the cold and dark, they spotted a number of horsemen on high ground to the south. They were still unsure at this stage where Argyll's main force was positioned. A party of horse and foot were sent to engage with the horsemen on the hill, but the horsemen turned away. Abandoning the pursuit, the Jacobite party returned to the main body of the army.

Three more hours were spent in inaction – it is likely that Mar was uncertain what to do while he still lacked definite knowledge of the location of the government troops. Eventually, after prolonged debate among the Jacobite commanders, it was decided that the army should move uphill in a southeasterly direction, ready for an attack. In order to reach high ground, the troops were moved from battle lines into columns. It was a procedure that was not without risk, for it made them vulnerable to attack, and therefore every effort was made to accomplish the move uphill at speed. The first line moved into two columns on the right and led by General Gordon, proceeded rapidly up the hill, accompanied by horsemen from the right wing of the army. The second line set off after them, also in two columns. Unfortunately, a speedy ascent was accomplished at the expense of order. The first two columns on the right wing moved very swiftly and the following columns could not catch up with them. To complicate matters further, the two companies of horse from the wings became displaced. The one which had been on the right arrived at the top of Sheriffmuir ridge between the two leading columns. The one from the left, which was the last body of troops to move from the original position, received confusing orders and instead of moving in a straight line, swung to the right, ending up on the wrong side of the army reassembling on the ridge at the top.

Meanwhile, at the other side of the hill, things were going none too well for Argyll. The party of horse appearing on the ridge earlier in the morning – and it is likely that he was among them – had been able to gather information about the size of the Jacobite army in comparison to their own. Taking their disadvantage in numbers into consideration, Argyll decided that the best policy was to move his men to the ridge, to give them the advantage of higher ground. Had they moved swiftly, this objective might have been achieved, but his army, cold, tired and sluggish after a night in the open, was too slow. As they were coming up one side of the hill, the Jacobites were coming up the other. As they struggled to get into fighting order on high ground, they realised that the Jacobites were moving in fast.

Both armies were only partially organised when the fighting commenced. Argyll's right wing, to the east, were almost prepared, but the left were still in disarray, facing an onslaught from the Jacobites' first line, under the command of General Gordon. The ferocity of the Highland charge was terrific. After firing an initial volley with their muskets, the Highlanders dived to the ground to avoid the bullets returning from the other side. While the government troops reloaded their weapons, the Highlanders rose and charged in an unstoppable mass, wielding their claymores. The force of it was irresistible and before long, the government troops were being driven back down the slope in a southerly direction. The Jacobites pursued them relentlessly, across the Wharry Burn in the valley at the foot of the hill. Mar was with this victorious body. When it was clear that the left wing of the government troops had been utterly destroyed, he regrouped his men and turned back up the hill.

While the Jacobite right wing had been successful, the left, under General Hamilton, had not fared so well. The right wing of the government army, under the command of Argyll himself, was much better organised. The Highlanders on the left of the Jacobite army fought with the same ferocity as those on the right, but they were met with well-disciplined resistance. After some time, Argyll brought the cavalry into play, sending them out and round to attack the Jacobite left flank. The cavalry charged the Highland lines several times, each time breaking them up more and driving them further back. Accounts of the battle differ, but it is thought that the left wing of the Jacobite army was without any cavalry support – the horse from the left wing, having been misdirected to the right, was not in a position to help. After three punishing hours of fighting, the Jacobite left had been driven right back to the east of Kinbuck, close to the Allan Water. Several Highlanders drowned in the waters of the river while trying to escape.

The battle had now become divided into two arenas, hundreds of yards apart. To the north, by Kinbuck, the Jacobites were facing humiliation. To the south, across the Wharry Burn, their forces had sent government survivors scurrying south with tales of defeat. In spite of the failure of his left flank, Mar was still in a superior position. He still had at least three times as many men under his command as Argyll had. Shortly after Mar had turned back to the place where the battle had begun, Argyll heard the news that his left flank had gone. He called in his troops from their pursuit of the Jacobites to the north of the battlefield and turned back to see what could be done to salvage the situation.

Mar's men had regrouped on a hillock at the eastern side of the battlefield. It is likely that there were almost 4000 Jacobite troops still in the field. The horsemen who had been misdirected before the main battle had now joined with the rest of the army. Argyll's comparatively meagre force – little more than a thousand men, were doubtless preparing themselves for the worst. They reformed less than quarter of a mile away, the cavalry on the wings, the infantry in the middle, their only other defence some earthen walls. The two sides faced up to each other for thirty minutes or so. Now was the time for Mar to show his mettle, to finish the battle in triumph, to proceed in victory through Stirling, across the Forth and towards the capital.

Inexplicably, he turned around and led his army away.

It may have been that Mar felt that victory was already his. It may have been that with darkness closing in, in spite of the numerical advantage that his army had, he decided that it was too risky to undertake further engagement. The Jacobites claimed that they had won the battle. Their losses were considerably less than those of the government. But how could victory be claimed when the other side had not capitulated – when the other side claimed victory itself? How could victory be claimed when the battle was stopped before it was over?

The Jacobite army spent the night some miles to the south. The next day, Argyll's men gathered up their dead and salvaged what weapons they could from the battlefield, unhindered by a party of watching Jacobites. The government army retired to Stirling, while Mar led his men back to Perth.

Whether he won or lost the battle, Mar's failure to follow through lost him the rising. The whole point of the engagement had been to overcome Argyll and take Stirling. Stirling was still in government hands and the chance of taking Scotland was now slipping from Mar's hands. And in as far as it was Mar's failure, it was Argyll's success, albeit at great cost.

After the Jacobite army returned to Perth, the situation grew worse. News reached the town that Inverness, which had been in Jacobite hands, had fallen to the Whigs, led by the earl of Sutherland with the assistance of Simon Fraser of Lovat. Now, through discontent and desertion, the Jacobite army began losing more men every day. The earls of Seaforth and Huntly both left Perth with their men at the beginning of December to return north to protect their own lands from the earl of Sutherland. By the end of February, both would have surrendered to the government.

CHAPTER TWENTY-SEVEN

The Arrival of the Pretender and the Death of the Rising

Since the days when the first plans had been formed for a rising on three fronts in England and Scotland, the Pretender had hoped, or at least intended, to make his landing in the southwest of England. Ormonde's flight to France did not prevent him from thinking that such a thing was possible. After the death of King Louis XIV, the situation in France became much more difficult for James. The duc D'Orleans, the French regent, remained firm in his resolve not to break with the terms of the Treaty of Utrecht and would not offer his support to the exiled king. He would not permit James to come to France. Nor would he allow himself to be put in a position where he could be accused of helping the Jacobite cause. It was Orleans who insisted that the duke of Berwick should not be permitted to go to Scotland. Furthermore, in September, when the English ambassador, the earl of Stair, had informed Orleans that a number of Jacobite ships were waiting in French ports, loaded with arms and supplies bound for Britain, Orleans had the ships unloaded and the cargoes confiscated.

In spite of Orleans' resolve to remain detached, James and Ormonde continued planning for James to sail from France to England to join the Jacobites. While the rising was being stamped out in southern England, while Mar was vacillating in Perth, while the Jacobites in the southwest of Scotland and northwest of England were quarrelling amongst themselves, losing credibility and heading towards Preston for the final debacle, James Francis Edward still held out hope for a landing in the south and a substantial show of support once he landed. Twice, Ormonde set sail from France to find a suitable landing-place for his master. Twice he returned, first from Plymouth, then from Cornwall, to report that a landing was impossible. Support in these places would no longer be forthcoming. The government had put paid to that.

It is strange that James took so long to abandon his plans for landing in England. We can only wonder at the quality and accuracy of communication between the Stewart court in the duchy of Lorraine and the Jacobites in both Scotland and England. Throughout his campaign, Mar was at first confident and then hopeful that James would be coming to Scotland with a large army, but this was never a likely prospect. Meanwhile, James was confident and then hopeful that he would be finding himself at the head of a successful rebellion in England. This prospect was just as unlikely. It took until the end of October for James to realise that his plans had to be changed and he would have to make his landing in Scotland. From Lorraine, he travelled first to Brittany. It was planned that he would sail from St Malo to Ireland and from there to Argyll. Unfortunately, this plan had to be abandoned when it was discovered that there were government troops in the area where James intended to land. His second option was to sail from Dunkirk to the northeast of Scotland. The wintry conditions made the journey to Dunkirk slow and difficult. The Pretender had to travel in disguise, for fear of capture or assassination. When he finally reached Dunkirk, it was the middle of December. The sea journey took several days – it was a small ship and the weather was atrocious. He had few men with him and no certain knowledge of the degree of support he could expect when he reached Scotland. He cannot have been feeling optimistic. When he finally arrived at Peterhead on 22 December, he would find that it was already too late.

Huntly and Seaforth were not the only deserters from Mar's army. The old problem of keeping Highlanders in service after battle had reared its head. Hundreds left to return to their homes. The Jacobite army was reduced by the time of the Pretender's arrival to a force of around 4000 men, considerably less than half its strength of two months earlier. In contrast to this, the government military position in Scotland was strengthening. Argyll's men in Stirling were joined by troops fresh from the victory at Preston and by the middle of December, the first battalions of 6000 troops from Holland had landed in the country. Things were looking progressively bleaker for the Jacobites. Mar himself had lost all optimism and had even made tentative overtures to Argyll regarding terms of capitulation. Nonetheless, when he heard that James was on his way, he had reassumed some of his former confidence and prepared to meet the Pretender with a cheerful countenance.

After landing, James sent an advance party to Perth while he travelled to Fetteresso Castle with a small band of supporters. He stayed at Fetteresso until 27 December, when Mar and a few other Jacobite leaders arrived to join him. He was due to leave for Perth almost immediately, but was struck down by a virus, which kept him confined to bed for several days. Finally, on 2 January, the royal party set out to make the journey to Perth, where a coronation was planned for him.

The Pretender's appearance, so long awaited, did not fulfil Jacobite hopes. With morale already dangerously low, their spirits must have sunk further when they learned that he had come without promise of men or arms from France. His poor state of health cannot have helped – nor his apparent lack of conviction and enthusiasm. The royal progress south from Fetteresso to Perth took seven days, but it was hardly a triumphal affair. The announcement that the rightful king's coronation would take place on 23 January at Scone was all but eclipsed by the news that Argyll's army in Stirling was steadily increasing and arming itself for a major attack on Perth.

In the end, the coronation had to be cancelled. On 21 January, a large party of Argyll's men was sent out on a reconnaissance mission towards Perth. News of their movements soon reached the Jacobites and caused immediate panic. Frantic attempts were made to fortify the town against attack. By 24 January, the Jacobites had news that Argyll had moved 3000 men from Stirling to Dunblane. In the certain knowledge that attack was imminent, the Jacobites resorted to desperate measures. Rather than making effective plans to meet the attack, they set about trying to hamper Argyll's progress. In the next few days, with the authority of the Pretender, parties were sent out to burn the villages on his route to Perth. The inhabitants were turned out of their homes into the snow, the buildings were set ablaze. Belongings were looted, provisions thrown into the fires. Auchterarder, Blackford, Crieff, Muthil and Dalreoch were all completely destroyed. It was a heartless act, leaving hundreds of people homeless and starving in the worst months of winter, and it would soon be proved that it had served no useful purpose whatsoever.

January was drawing to a close and the Jacobite army's plans were still uncertain. Argyll would make his move soon – should they stay and fight, or retreat? Opinions were divided – one side thought that a retreat would amount to nothing less than outright cowardice, whilst others, including Mar, and under his influence, James Francis Edward, thought that a withdrawal was the only realistic option. After a prolonged council of war, Mar's pessimism prevailed. The decision was taken in the full knowledge that in abandoning Perth, the Jacobites were effectively bringing the rising to an end. There were no plans to turn at a later stage and fight again. The only problem they faced now was making a safe retreat.

The Jacobite army evacuated Perth just in time. Argyll's progress had not been unduly hampered by the scorched earth policy and in spite of the harsh weather conditions, his army arrived in the town only the day after the Jacobites left. From Perth, the Jacobites proceeded to Dundee and then Montrose, with Argyll following behind. On 5 February, a day after the arrival of the Jacobite army in Montrose, the Pretender was secreted onto a ship bound for France. Most of his followers were unaware of his departure – plans for his escape had deliberately been kept a secret to avoid the risk of a mutiny – but among those who accompanied him was the earl of Mar. After successfully evading government vessels that were patrolling the waters close by, the ship, the *Marie Therese,* bore the Pretender and the hopes of his followers away from Scotland. Many of the Jacobites were enraged when they found out. James had left a letter, which was read out to them two days after his departure. In it, he expressed his regret at the failure of the rising, but stressed his concern for the safety of his followers. He reasoned that it was better to retire to France to await another opportunity to support his countrymen in a rising at a later date, under more favourable conditions. In spite of James' protestations of good intent, there were many Jacobites who felt that they had been badly let down by a weak-willed and cowardly leader.

Marshal Keith and General Gordon were left to oversee the rest of the retreat. Gordon took the lead, while Keith took command of the rearguard. From Montrose, the remnants of the Jacobite army moved to Stonehaven, then on to Aberdeen, Inverury, Strathbogie, and Keith. All along the way, men were leaving. A number of officers managed to escape on ships from Peterhead and Fraserburgh. Other men quietly slipped away when the opportunity presented itself. The possibility of joining forces with Huntly and attacking Inverness was quietly raised. Huntly would take no part in it. The last of the troops continued to Strathdon, then to Strathspey. At Ruthven in Badenoch, General Gordon had a last meeting with the remaining clansmen, and the final dispersal took place. While many of the more important figures sought refuge where they could – the Western Isles, France, Sweden – the clansmen quietly made their way home. Argyll's pursuit had already been brought to an end. He followed the Jacobites only as far as Aberdeen. Although his army had followed Mar's closely all the way from Perth, it had never moved fast enough to catch them up and engage with them. Argyll was under suspicion of letting his sympathies for fellow Scots get the better of him. He was accused of wanting to show leniency to the rebels. At the end of February, he was removed from his position and General William Cadogan took over command of the government army. In spite of his efforts on behalf of the government, Argyll ended the rebellion in disgrace.

The survivors of the 1715 rising in Scotland undoubtedly fared better than their fellow rebels in England. Most of the leaders had the time to make good their escape, either into exile or into remote parts of their own country. Most of those who had submitted, including Huntly, were kept prisoner for some time but were eventually released. An Act of Attainder in 1716 named 39 Scottish nobles, many of whom were by this time safely abroad, and caused their estates to be forfeited. In order to keep peace in the country, garrisons were established in Edinburgh, Glasgow, Stirling, Perth Dundee, Aberdeen, Montrose, and a number of other towns. More than 70 prisoners of the rebellion languished in jails in Edinburgh and elsewhere for a number of months while the government debated how their cases might be dealt with. It seemed unlikely that they would be convicted in a Scottish court. Eventually, amidst out- rage, they were transported to Carlisle to await trial under English law – a contravention of the terms of the Treaty of Union. Fortunately, most were eventually released without charge and none were executed.

The government forces were less than vigorous in their efforts to ensure that the Highlands were subdued after the rising. A Disarming Act passed in 1716 was barely enforced – the authorities seemed satisfied that their aims had been achieved when the clan chiefs handed over comparatively few weapons in poor condition. Amnesty would be granted in return for submission. As long as the clan chiefs paid lip service to the idea of surrender, their word was accepted. General Cadogan stayed only a few months in Scotland after the rebellion was over. As long as there was an appearance of calm restored, he saw no reason to take further action.

Chapter Twenty-Eight

The Rebellion of 1719

The failure of the 1715 rebellion was indeed a sorry one, but, nonetheless, it had not dimmed the hopes of committed Jacobites. The plotting continued. The problem of motivating Jacobite followers in Britain – in particular, those in England – without concrete promise of foreign military and financial support remained a stumbling block. Since the death of Louis XIV in 1714, hopes of France giving its backing to a Jacobite rising had dwindled to nothing. France and England were now at peace and France was unwilling to break the terms of the Treaty of Utrecht without provocation.

In 1716, under pressure from Britain, the duke of Lorraine was obliged to ask James to leave and the Jacobite court moved to the papal territory of Avignon, in the south of France. Its stay there was destined to be short-lived, and in response to further threats from Britain, Pope Clement XI was compelled to invite James to move to Italy in 1717.

In 1718, hopes of a Jacobite rebellion began to soar again, this time with the help of Spain. Once again, a foreign power was willing to assist the Jacobite cause for its own ends. Spain, still smarting from the Treaty of Utrecht, in which it had lost considerable territory, was in conflict with Britain over interests in Italy and the Netherlands and looking for a diversion. Causing grief on British soil offered them the perfect opportunity of such a diversion. Cardinal Alberoni, first minister of Spain, offered Spanish backing for another Jacobite rebellion in England. Arms would be provided, a force of Spanish regular troops and ships to transport them. The Pretender, the duke of Ormonde, Earl Marischal and his brother, James, travelled to Madrid to discuss Alberoni's ideas. His offer of help was gladly accepted, but with some alteration to his proposed plans. The duke of Ormonde, who was to be given command of the invasion, suggested a two-pronged attack, with the main force landing in England and a smaller, diversionary force, landing on the west coast of Scotland. Ormonde was no doubt remembering the potential for valuable support from the Highland clans when he suggested this. Additionally, there were still a great many government soldiers stationed around Scotland and it was sensible to keep them occupied there rather than have them diverted to England to threaten the success of an invasion there.

After some haggling, Ormonde persuaded Alberoni to supply an army of 5000 men, some cannon and enough arms for an army of 15,000 men for the landing in England, which Ormonde himself would lead. Earl Marischal was to lead the landing in Scotland. Marischal's allocated resources were considerably smaller, amounting to approximately 300 Spanish foot soldiers and arms for 2000 men. The Pretender was to accompany Ormonde's expedition. It was arranged that the main fleet – 29 ships in total – would assemble at Cadiz before sailing to Corunna. There, they would pick up James Francis Edward and stock up supplies before setting off for England. The smaller fleet was to sail from San Sebastian.

The main fleet set sail from Cadiz at the end of the first week in March 1719, but soon fell prey to ill-fortune. Sailing round Cape Finisterre at the end of the month, they were caught up in bad weather. So fierce were the storms that hit them that some of the ships sank, and many more, badly damaged, were forced to turn back or make a landing in nearby ports. Only a few made it as far as Cadiz. The Pretender, meanwhile, who was making his way to Corunna from Italy, suffered similarly from the weather. His crossing of the Mediterranean took much longer than had been anticipated. By the time he had made it from Italy, via

Madrid, to Corunna, he had been travelling for several weeks. As it happened, his late arrival was of no consequence. With the fleet all but destroyed, plans for the invasion of England had been abandoned.

Meanwhile, unaware that anything was wrong, Keith's little force had set sail from San Sebastian on 8 March and made it safely to the Hebrides. There, in Stornoway on the island of Lewis, Keith's fleet was joined by some other Jacobite exiles, including the marquis of Tullibardine, General Gordon, the earl of Seaforth and a few others. Keith's brother, James, had travelled to Le Havre to recruit them and bring them over to Scotland. Almost at once a dispute arose between Keith and the marquis of Tullibardine over leadership. Tullibardine had a document proving that he had been appointed commander of the Jacobites in Scotland and although Keith was reluctantly forced to accept this, he claimed authority over the vessels that had been brought over from Spain. And whilst Tullibardine proposed a more cautious plan of action, and wanted to wait for news of Ormonde's landing in England before landing on the mainland, Keith was in favour of making a quick strike on the garrison at Inverness before news of their presence reached the government.

Eventually, it was agreed that a landing should be made on the mainland, but the site was changed. The small fleet sailed into Loch Alsh and the troops set up headquarters in Eilean Donan Castle. Before taking further action, it was decided that they should wait for news of Ormonde and take steps to rally further support. Messages were sent out to neighbouring clans and further afield to members of the nobility to the south who were known to be sympathetic to the Jacobite cause.

The government had been aware for some time that plans were afoot for an invasion and were already taking steps to put an end to it. The British navy was alerted and warships sent up to the west coast of Scotland.

After a period of anxious waiting, the Jacobites got word of the failure of Ormonde's expedition. The division between the two leaders grew deeper, with Tullibardine insisting that the enterprise be called off, whilst Keith refused to contemplate the idea of giving up. In order to prevent Tullibardine from returning to Spain, Keith ordered the Spanish ships away, giving him no option but to stay. Tullibardine's response was to redouble his efforts to summon support. The Spanish ships sailed off just before a fleet of five English ships arrived. In Eilean Donan Castle, the meagre garrison of 45 Spanish troops guarding the Jacobite arms and ammunition now found themselves under bombardment. The castle was blown up and whatever stores and ammunition were not destroyed were captured.

Marischal was compelled to withdraw inland. By this time a force of more than 1000 men had assembled, most of whom were Seaforth Mackenzies and Macgregors led by Rob Roy, in addition to approximately 250 Spanish troops. Unfortunately, the time spent waiting for news from Ormonde had given the government time to mobilise not only its ships, but also a land force. General Wightman was making his way down the Great Glen from Inverness with a large body of men. The two armies met at Glen Shiel. The Jacobite army moved into the glen and blocked it off at a point where it narrowed. They spread out across the valley and up the steep slope to the north. Wightman's force was smaller, but he deployed them carefully. He had the advantage of heavy mortars with him and he used them to deadly effect, blasting the Highlanders from their positions before they had time to charge upon his men. Mortar fire was followed by an advance on foot by his grenadiers. The grenades that were hurled into the lines of Jacobites caused immediate confusion and almost at once, many of them began to retreat. There was little, if any, hand-to hand fighting. The clansmen that survived the initial onslaught made good their escape and disappeared into the wilds. After an initial brave stand, the Spaniards, with nowhere else to go and the Scots deserting them, lost heart and surrendered as prisoners of war.

All of the Jacobite leaders escaped capture, but their reputations had been tarnished by the failure of the enterprise. The Spanish troops who had been taken prisoner were eventually repatriated.

The offer of military support from Spain would not come again. Spain was doing badly in the war and, by the autumn of 1719, Philip was forced to negotiate terms for peace. Ormond and James left Spain. It had been the Pretender's last chance for claiming the throne for himself. The next rebellion, 26 years later, would be the task of a son who had not yet been conceived.

CHAPTER TWENTY-NINE

Between 1719 and 1745

In 1719, the Jacobite court transferred to Rome. In the same year, after protracted negotiations, James was married to the Polish princess, Clementina Sobieska. Two sons were born to the couple, in spite of the fact that the marriage was less than happy. In 1720, Charles Edward was born and his brother Henry was born in 1725.

Life in Rome was reasonably comfortable for the Jacobite court. The pope provided James with a generous pension and they were comfortably accommodated at the Palazzo Muti. Even the Protestant followers of the Pretender found a tolerant welcome in the papal territory. They were permitted to follow their own religion in private – something they had not had the freedom to do in Lorraine.

In Scotland meanwhile, measures were being taken to reduce the risk of further trouble from the rebellious Highland clans. Much of the difficulty in maintaining law and order in remoter regions of the country was down to the fact that the terrain was difficult and there were no routes from place to place that were easily traversable in rough weather. These conditions had been used historically by the Highlanders to their own advantage – their ability to move swiftly over difficult ground in all weathers had been part of their particular strength as a fighting force. It had proved invaluable in the campaigns of Montrose. It had kept them out of reach of General Mackay in the months leading up to the battle of Killiecrankie. More recently, it had kept them safe from the advance of Argyll's army in the retreat from Perth after the failure of the '15 rebellion. In order for the government to turn the situation back to their own advantage, communications in the Highlands had to be improved.

The task of pacifying the Highlands was given to General Wade. After making a careful study, Wade decided that improvements should concentrate on policing the Highlands properly, fortifying government outposts in the Highlands and facilitating easier and quicker movement between the government outposts. Firstly, the government had to have properly trained manpower distributed throughout the Highlands, led by men who spoke the Gaelic tongue and knew the locality. Men had to be recruited and trained specifically for the purpose of representing the government's interests, enforcing a new Disarming Act and policing these unruly areas. Six independent companies of men were raised in 1725 and distributed throughout the Highlands. In 1739, four more were added and the ten companies were formed into the 42nd (Highland) Regiment of Foot, the Black Watch. Between 1719 and 1745, forts were expanded and strengthened. By 1745, there were significant military presences at three key points down the Great Glen – at Inverness, Fort Augustus and Fort William. Additionally, there were forts at Bernera on the west coast, Inversnaid by Loch Lomond and Ruthven Barracks by Kingussie. In order to improve communications, Wade began a programme of road and bridge construction. A new, improved road was built down the Great Glen, linking Fort William, Fort Augustus and Inverness. Inverness and Ruthven Barracks were also linked by part of a road that ran from Dunkeld to Dalwhinnie and on to Inverness. Branches of this road led from Dalnacardoch across the Tummel and the Tay to Amulree and from Dalwhinnie across the Corrieyairack Pass to Fort Augustus.

It was a period of relative calm in Scotland, but the Jacobite cause had not been forgotten.

CHAPTER THIRTY

1744: Rebellion Has a Difficult Birth

There was a distinct slump in Jacobite activity after the failure of the 1719 rising. The Pretender seemed almost content to continue living in exile in Rome. He had never been a man of strong constitution, and few people believed he had the strength of mind or of will to lead another attempt to claim the thrones of Britain. The Jacobites still believed they had a cause to fight for, but with an ageing, inactive figurehead and no hope of foreign aid, there was little they could do.

In 1740, the War of the Austrian Succession broke out and the situation began to change. Louis XV was finding the conflict a great drain on his resources. As his father had done before him, he began to see the value in supporting a Jacobite rising in Britain for his own ends. Invading Britain with a French army, thus declaring war against them, would necessitate the diversion of British troops from Belgium and Holland. After protracted negotiations with the Pretender, it was eventually decided in 1744 that an invasion of both Scotland and England would be made, commanded by Marshal Saxe. The young Prince Charles Edward Stewart, now a sturdy, strong-willed young man of 24 years, would represent his father on the expedition. Charles travelled from Rome to Paris in February 1744; while, in France, a fleet of ships was made ready to carry 15,000 troops over to Britain. Only one fifth of these was destined for Scotland. The remaining 12,000 were to land on English shores, ready to march on London.

The expedition never left port. The British had received intelligence that an invasion was planned, and were already mobilising ships of the Royal Navy to oppose it, but it was the weather that finally put paid to the French plans. Severe storms blew up before the ships had even left port, causing massive damage. The French lost heart and the expedition was abandoned, much to the frustration of the young Prince Charles.

Instead of returning to Rome, Charles remained in Paris after the expedition of 1744 had been aborted, trying to persuade Louis XV to give his backing to another attempt, but his efforts met with no success. In Paris, he gathered round him a body of acquaintances sympathetic to the Jacobite cause, many of whom were Irish Jacobites. There were still a number of exiled Jacobites in France, with whom the Prince was in contact. He was also aware of the fact that prominent Jacobites in Scotland had pledged their support to the proposed invasion of 1744 and that there was also a large number of Jacobite sympathisers in England, particularly in the north. Charles was determined to attempt a rising and claim the throne for his father. If he could not count on French assistance from the outset, then he must mount an expedition on his own in the hope that once the rising was underway, French help would be forthcoming.

Amongst Charles's acquaintances was Anthony Walsh, an Irish Jacobite and a shipowner. With his help, the prince managed to get hold of two vessels for the expedition – a 68-gun frigate called the *Elisabeth* and a smaller 20-gun frigate called the *Du Teillay*. The *Du Teillay* was anchored at St Nazaire, near Nantes. The *Elisabeth,* after being loaded at Brest with weapons procured by Charles and some supplies and money, would join her at Belle Isle before the expedition set off. The weapons assembled for the expedition amounted to 20 cannon, 1500 muskets, and 1100 broadswords. There was also a quantity of ammunition. Charles had been careful to keep the expedition preparations secret from his father. In order to raise the funds to buy weapons, he had had to ask his father to sell some jewellery on his behalf, but he had not been entirely honest about his reasons for needing the money. He knew that James would never have allowed him to take such a dangerous gamble without the help of the French. Only when everything was ready for departure did Charles write his father a letter from Navarre, explaining and justifying his actions. He also wrote a letter to Louis XV, which stated that although he had undertaken the project alone, he trusted that the French king would see the benefit of lending his help to it. A third letter was sent to the duchess of Salas, asking her to use her influence to enlist the support of the Spanish court.

The two ships set sail from Belle Ile on 12 July. Charles was on board the smaller ship, the *Du Teillay,* along with seven companions: the duke of Atholl (or marquis of Tullibardine as he was known to the Whigs), the Reverend George Kelly, Aeneas Macdonald, Sir John Macdonnell, John William O'Sullivan, Sir Thomas Sheridan and Francis Strickland. On the *Elisabeth* were approximately 100 men from the Irish regiment of St Claire. It was hardly an impressive assembly with which to challenge the security of the house of Hanover, but this, along with his meagre supply of weaponry and a fund of 400 Louis D'Or, was all that Charles had.

The two ships had only been at sea for a few days when disaster struck. A British ship, HMS *Lion,* sailed into their path and engaged the *Elisabeth* in battle. Prince Charles, on board the *Du Teillay,* could only watch helplessly as the *Elisabeth* was pounded by cannon fire from the *Lion*. The battle lasted several hours. Both ships were severely damaged. The captain of the *Elisabeth* was killed and his ship, hopelessly damaged, forced to turn back to port. The young prince had lost his soldiers and some of his arms. The enterprise, which had at first seemed reckless, now appeared to be a lost cause. Nonetheless, undaunted, the *Du Teillay* sailed on. Prince Charles finally reached Scotland in the third week of July. The *Du Teillay* anchored by the tiny island of Eriskay and on 23 July, the prince stepped onto Scottish soil for the first time.

Charles spent his first night in the home of a tacksman, Angus Macdonald. Nothing could have been further removed from the comforts of court life in Italy, but the prince was undeterred.

His reception was not encouraging. One of the first men to meet him after his landing was Alexander Macdonald of Boisdale, brother of Macdonald of Clanranald, who was brought from Uist to speak with him. Boisdale was of the opinion that no one would be prepared to rise for a prince who had come without men or arms and that Charles should turn back for France while he still had the chance. Boisdale brought word from Alexander Macdonald of Sleat and Norman Macleod of Macleod that they were both of the same opinion. This surprised the prince, who had been under the impression that Macleod in particular had offered his unconditional support. But he had come too far to be put off. He returned to the *Du Teillay* and they sailed to the mainland, putting down anchor in Loch nan Uamh near Moidart. The prince's intention now was to seek the help of Kinlochmoidart, brother of Aeneas Macdonald. Kinlochmoidart was sent for and when he came, he was accompanied by Macdonald of Clanranald. They were then joined by the young Clanranald, Clanranald's son. After protracted discussions with the prince, first Kinlochmoidart and then Clanranald reluctantly offered their support. With their help, word went out and the men began to gather – a number of other Macdonalds, including Macdonald of Glenaladale and Macdonald of Keppoch pledged their support.

One chief upon whom the prince had been counting for support was Donald Cameron of Lochiel, whose family had longstanding loyalty to the Stewarts and whose father had been attainted after the rising of 1715. Lochiel came to see Charles in person, not, to the prince's surprise and disappointment, to commit himself to the cause, but to try to dissuade him from proceeding any further. Charles's powers of persuasion were considerable. Lochiel's initial reluctance to join the prince's army disappeared as soon as his loyalty was questioned. In persuading Lochiel, whose influence was considerable, Charles had won a major coup. If Lochiel had refused to join him, others would undoubtedly have withheld their support for the campaign. Word was sent to Murray of Broughton, who had pledged his support for the Jacobite rebellion supported by the French invasion, that the prince had come and he, Murray, was expected to live up to his promises. He appeared in the camp in the middle of August and was appointed Charles's secretary. Gradually, as the leaders were won round, their men followed.

A council of war was held and it was decided that, on 19 August, the standard would be raised at Glenfinnan. By the time Charles left Moidart to move on to Glenfinnan, he had high hopes. But already the problem of supplying his men with food was raising its head. After a clever piece of piracy by Anthony Walsh, barley and oatmeal were procured from two ships offshore and the booty was divided between the men. In spite of this unexpected bonus, there were precious few provisions to feed an army in the longer term and very little money to buy more with. It was a sign of things to come. Hunger would follow Charlie's army for much of their campaign.

The raising of the Stewart standard proved to be unexpectedly morale-boosting. On their way to Glenfinnan, Macdonald of Keppoch and his men had encountered and surrounded two companies of government soldiers, who were travelling from Fort Augustus to Fort William to reinforce the garrison there. The soldiers had been so terrified by the sight and sound of the Highlanders that they had surrendered with barely a murmur. It was the first victory of the campaign and it had been won without loss of life on the Jacobites' side. The prisoners were brought to Glenfinnan and offered the chance of fighting for Charles, but they refused. In spite of this, they were treated with courtesy by the young prince.

To add to the clansmen already assembled, most of whom were Macdonalds, Keppoch had brought 300 more men to Glenfinnan. Macdonald of Morar brought 150 more. Clan Cameron came out in force, with around 700 men marching up to the assembly point to the skirl of bagpipes. Last to arrive were some more men rounded up by the young Clanranald. The army now amounted to around 1300 men, but although this was a modest start, the mood was optimistic. After the royal proclamation had been read to the assembly by Tullibardine, the company gave itself up to celebration.

The Jacobite army moved on from Glenfinnan, carefully avoiding Fort William, to Lochgarry Castle. The British government, incredulous at first at the news that Charles had landed in the country without an army, was hastily gathering what troops it could muster under the command of Sir John Cope. It was not easy to find enough men, for most of the army was engaged in fighting abroad in the War of the Austrian Succession. Less than 4000 remained in Scotland, and they were scattered in different places. Cope was not prepared in time for an assault at Glenfinnan, but while the Jacobite army was moving to Lochgarry, Cope's army had begun moving north from Stirling.

The young prince was kept well informed of Cope's movements and was aware, at Lochgarry, that Cope was marching to meet him. Cope's army was heading from Stirling, north to Crieff and from there, progressing along the road built by Wade through Amulree, to Dalwhinnie. From there they would head towards Fort Augustus, through the Corrieyairack Pass. The Jacobites reacted swiftly and headed towards Corrieyairack, ready to block the road and intercept Cope's army.

Many of Cope's men were untrained, and by the time they reached Dalnacardoch, they were already tired from the march from Stirling. Cope had held out hope that his force would be augmented en route by several hundred Highlanders from the estates of the duke of Atholl, Tullibardine's brother, who was loyal to the government. Unfortunately, wherever the duke's loyalties might lie, his men, for the most part, supported the Jacobites and the attainted Tullibardine. Consequently, none came out to support Cope. In addition to all this, supporters of Charles had cleverly misinformed the general that the Jacobite force was twice its actual size. In these circumstances, Cope decided to avoid a confrontation at Corrieyairack. His army turned northwest at Dalwhinnie and headed for Ruthven Barracks, en route for Inverness. Cope's plan was possibly to gather reinforcements at Inverness and move down the Great Glen to attack the Jacobite army there, or to travel back south to Edinburgh by sea. However, no matter how swiftly he forced his men to march, he could not be quick enough.

His change of plan had laid the way open for the Jacobite army to move south and they wasted no time. Their numbers had already swelled – after some persuasion, Cluny Macpherson had agreed to bring his men to join the Jacobites under Prince Charles. They moved on to Blair Castle, arriving there at the beginning of September, and were given a wonderful reception. The duke had left when he heard of the movements of the Jacobite army and the men of Atholl were pleased to welcome the elderly Tullibardine back to the family home he had been absent from for thirty years. At Blair, the prince discovered that a number of the clansmen had absented themselves from the army. Denied of the immediate prospect of battle and looting by Cope's diversion, they had lost heart and were heading for home. The problem of leading a force of Highlanders was not new to the Scots, but it was new to the prince. Men were sent out to bring the deserters back by whatever means necessary.

The army set off from Blair Castle well rested and fed, and proceeded to Perth. Charles led his men into the city on 4 September, to a mixed reception. At Perth, the size of the army increased again and two more leaders were recruited by Charles. Lord James Drummond, recognised by Jacobites but not by Whigs as the duke of Perth, joined up, as did another brother of the duke of Atholl, Lord George Murray. Drummond's health was not good, and he lacked experience in military matters, but his enthusiasm and courage went some way towards compensating for these failings. Lord George Murray, in comparison, had both experience and talent as a military leader. He was a good deal younger than Tullibardine, his frail elder brother, and had proven his loyalty to the prince's father twice already, in the campaigns of 1715 and 1719. Some years after the rising of 1719, however, Murray had made peace with the government and had been pardoned. This, in the eyes of some Jacobites, including Charles, was reason to suspect his motives. Nonetheless, although he was not universally popular among the ranks of the Jacobites, Murray's competency as a leader was never in question. Charles gave both Murray and Drummond the rank of Lieutenant-General, but it was Murray who assumed overall leadership of the army. The relationship between Murray and the prince was not destined to be an easy one – Charles was irritated by Murray's arrogance while Murray, for his part, did not have faith in the prince's skills as a military tactician.

In Perth, Charles turned his attention to the urgent problem of raising funds for his army. Taxes were levied in the city and collectors sent to other towns to do the same. The money was not always paid willingly, but what was collected went some way towards funding the next stage of the enterprise. For a few days, the army remained in the city, but the leaders were always conscious of the need to move on while they still had the advantage.

CHAPTER THIRTY-ONE

The Jacobites Move to Edinburgh

On 11 September, Charles's army was on the march again and headed through Dunblane. After camping close to Dunblane for two nights, they continued. They crossed the Forth at the Fords of Frew near Stirling. An expected confrontation at the river crossing did not take place. A company of dragoons under the command of Colonel Gardiner, which was supposed to be guarding the crossing, and which the Jacobites were fully prepared to meet, withdrew before their arrival and the Jacobites crossed unopposed. The following day, the army bypassed Stirling Castle, avoiding canon fire from the garrison that had been left there, and marched on to Falkirk, where the prince spent the night of 14 September enjoying the hospitality of the earl of Kilmarnock at Callander House.

While at Callander House, Charles received intelligence that Gardiner's dragoons, after their withdrawal from Stirling, had now moved to Linlithgow and were intent on disputing the Jacobite army's crossing of the bridge at Linlithgow. The prince sent a contingent of men forthwith to deal with them, but for a second time, Gardiner's men withdrew, this time to Kirkliston, a few miles out of Edinburgh, and then to Linlithgow. The next day, Charles led his army on to join the advance party at Linlithgow, where he was welcomed and lavishly entertained at the palace for a few hours. The army moved out in the late afternoon and camped for the night a few miles to the east of the town. On the morning of 16 September, the prince led his men on towards Edinburgh.

The capital was poorly prepared for the arrival of the Jacobite army. The castle itself was well-defended and well-provisioned, but the rest of the city had neither the means nor the organisation to mount any sort of effective defence. In the city itself, half-hearted and ineffectual defensive measures had been taken. Extra volunteers had been called in to reinforce the town guard, but as a fighting force, the guard lacked both conviction and leadership, and the men called up to volunteer to join them could not be persuaded to move outside the city walls to face the Jacobites. Colonel Gardiner's dragoons, having withdrawn east from Kirkliston, had joined up with another company under the command of Colonel Hamilton and had positioned themselves at Coltbridge, a couple of miles from the city itself. The town guard, minus its faint-hearted volunteers, amounted to little over 100 men. They joined Gardiner and Hamilton's men at Coltbridge, ready to face the Jacobite advance.

In the event, the encounter was a farce. At the first sight of the Jacobite vanguard, the first line of the dragoons turned around and fled. The panic spread to the entire body of defenders who promptly made off to the east of the city, abandoning the capital to its fate.

The sight of the undignified retreat of Gardiner and Hamilton's dragoons further damaged morale in Edinburgh. The city authorities decided that the time had come to bargain. A letter received from the prince, who was now encamped at Slateford, approximately two miles west of the city, called upon the town council to ensure that the Jacobites could enter the city peacefully. In return, the prince promised to guarantee the rights and liberties of the citizens of Edinburgh. A deputation was sent out that evening to the Jacobite camp to discuss terms. But the prince was in no mood for bargaining. The gates of the city were to be opened to his army, or they would be compelled to use force. A second delegation was sent out in the early hours of the morning of 17 September and received much the same response. Charles was aware that time was running out if he was to take the city without a struggle. Cope's army was likely to be on its way to relieve the capital.

After the second deputation had been sent on its way, the prince sent parties of men out from the camp to see whether they could enter any of the city gates by stealth. An attempt to gain entry at the Netherbow Port, whereby a man disguised as a dragoon tried to persuade the guard to open the gates, failed. Then fortune took a hand. The carriage that had taken the second delegation out to the Jacobite camp had dropped its passengers off within the city walls and was now returning to stables in the Canongate. The gates were opened to allow it through and the Jacobites waiting nearby took their chance and rushed through. Once inside the city, it did not take them long to overpower the guards at the other gates and other strategic points.

When dawn broke, the city was in Jacobite hands. Only the castle remained outwith their control. News of the capture of Edinburgh was conveyed to Charles at Slateford with all speed. The prince left Slateford with the remainder of his army and taking a route to the south of the city to avoid the danger of fire from the castle, entered the King's Park, in the shadow of Arthur's Seat, and took up possession of Holyrood House. In the early afternoon, at the Mercat Cross in the High Street, the prince's father was proclaimed King James VIII of Scotland.

CHAPTER THIRTY-TWO

The Battle of Prestonpans

Fye now, Johnny, get up and run,
The Highland bagpipes mak' a din,
It's better tae sleep in a hale skin,
For 't will be a bloody morning.
                    'Hey Johnny Cope' – Jacobite Song

The taking of the capital city had been a real stroke of luck and had been achieved in the nick of time. Cope's army had sailed south from Aberdeen and was now landing at Dunbar. On landing, they were joined by the troops who had taken part in the shameful retreat from Coltbridge, which would become known as the 'Canter of Coltbrig'. From Dunbar, Cope's army moved to Haddington. Hearing of Cope's arrival, Charles moved his army to Duddingston, a short distance to the south east of the city. On 19 September, in a house in Duddingston, he held a council of war. His army had been reinforced by a good number of new recruits on the journey south. After the taking of Edinburgh, morale was high. They were ready for a battle. From Duddingston, the Jacobites marched on the next day, crossing the River Esk by the old bridge at Musselburgh,* and moving towards Tranent. Intelligence had reached them that Cope's army was also on the move and was in the vicinity of Prestonpans. This was confirmed when the Jacobites were approaching Tranent. Cope's army was positioned about a mile to the north of them, between the village of Preston and Seton House. Between the two armies lay a stretch of boggy ground, which would make it very difficult for the Highland army. Any attempt at a Highland charge across this kind of terrain would be hopelessly slowed down.

It was late in the day and accordingly, the armies of both sides made camp for the night where they were. Battle would have to be postponed until the next day. Once again, fortune favoured the Jacobites. Late at night word was brought to the Jacobite leaders of a man who knew a route through the marshlands. Using this route, the Jacobite army could move round the Hanoverian army and attack it from the east, on the left flank. In the darkest hours of the night, the prince's army was roused and led in silence, often in single file, across the marshes. As dawn began to break, the army's movements were still concealed by a heavy mist that had fallen the night before. The Hanoverians slept while the Jacobites formed themselves up ready for battle. The Macdonald clan were on the right wing, commanded by the duke of Perth. On the left wing, Lord George Murray took command of the Camerons and Stewarts of Appin. The centre positions were taken by Macgregors and the duke of Perth's regiment. Behind this grouping, which stood as the front line of attack, were arranged the men of Atholl, the Robertsons, the Macdonalds of Glencoe and the Maclachlans. When the Hanoverians awoke the next morning, it was to the news that their enemy was within less than half a mile of them and coming from an unexpected direction.

Hastily, the Hanoverian troops were turned about to face the forthcoming attack. The armies were relatively evenly matched in terms of numbers but the prince's army now had the advantage in the element of surprise. They were now at close quarters with the Hanoverians and could make full use of the ferocious Highland charge. The mist that still hung in patches over the battlefield meant that many of the Hanoverians could not see their attackers until they were within 200 yards of them. The Highland advance was a little untidy. Marshy ground to the south slowed down the left flank as it advanced. But nothing was lost from this. The Highlanders fired their muskets as they came within range of the enemy, then flung them aside and rushed full-tilt through the enemy gunfire with swords, daggers and targes at the ready. Fending off the bayonet thrusts of the Hanoverian soldiers with their targes in their left hands, they wielded their swords in their right hands with deadly effect. The Camerons were the first to engage with the enemy, sending most of Gardiner's dragoons, who were on the Hanoverian right wing, into terrified flight. Deserted by his men, Colonel Gardiner stood his ground with a few stalwarts, but was killed. On the left wing of the Hanoverian army, Hamilton's dragoons, equally cowardly, turned and ran. The onslaught was relentless thereafter and the battle was over in a very short time.

More than 500 Hanoverians were killed and several hundred were taken prisoner. In contrast, losses on the Jacobite side were extremely light, with only 30 or 40 men killed and less than a hundred wounded. Cope managed to escape from the battlefield with around 400 dragoons. They made their way to Coldstream and then to Berwick with news of the terrible defeat. The Camerons meanwhile had made their way back to Edinburgh with the tidings of the prince's great victory. Charles expressed his wish that Cope be pursued to Berwick, but was advised that such a course of action was too risky at this point. He spent the night at Pinkie House in Musselburgh before returning to Edinburgh. The next day, the main body of his army processed triumphantly back into the city and the prince resumed residence in Holyrood House.

In the next few weeks, Charles divided his time between hosting balls at Holyrood and talking in council with his leaders. A messenger was sent south to alert English Jacobites to the prince's success in Scotland and to rally their support, but he was captured at Newcastle. Another messenger was sent to France to ask for the French king's commitment to the cause with troops and arms. Already divisions were beginning to appear between the supporters of Lord George Murray and those closest to the prince. Charles was intent on progressing south and to this end, he was making determined efforts to raise more men from the Highlands to swell his army. He was convinced that his army's arrival in England would be enough to bring out the English Jacobites in support, enabling him to proceed to London and take control of the country. Lord George Murray, on the other hand, was reluctant to proceed any further without a guarantee of men and munitions from France and proba-bly realised that the English Jacobites would share his sentiments.

After the beginning of October, the Jacobite army began to grow. Lord Ogilvie, son of the earl of Airlie, arrived with around 600 clansmen. John Gordon of Glenbucket arrived on 4 October with another 400 men. Lord Pitsligo brought men from Aberdeenshire, including more than 100 cavalry, a welcome addition to the Jacobite army, which was sadly lacking in horsemen. In addition to these, more Highlanders joined the clans already present in the prince's army and from the northern highlands, John Lewis Gordon, brother of the duke of Gordon, brought several hundred more men. By the end of October, the Jacobite army numbered around 6000 men. Charles was ready and determined to take the rising into the next stage and advance into England.

Lord George Murray, aware that the government had had ample time to organise troops to retaliate against the threat of the insur-gents, urged caution. His preference was for a tactical withdrawal into the Highlands, terrain upon which the large proportion of the Jacobite army was accustomed to fighting and upon which they would have the advantage. It would be unlikely that government troops would follow them there and if they did, the Jacobites would have the greater chance of success. Moving north and hopefully stalling a major confrontation would allow time for much-needed support from France to materialise. The prince, however, was not willing to listen. His argument won the day and at length it was agreed that they would advance south. They would avoid a direct advance on Newcastle. Marshal Wade had assembled a considerable force of government cavalry and infantry in Newcastle and was in a strong, well-defended position. If they avoided a direct attack on Wade, they might succeed in bringing him out to face him in a posi-tion where the Highland army was better placed to secure a victory. The army prepared to move out at the beginning of November. They moved from Edinburgh to Dalkeith, where they spent a cou-ple of nights, then they divided into two divisions for the march south.

CHAPTER THIRTY-THREE

The Advance into England

Splitting the army in two was a tactical decision to confuse the enemy, leaving them uncertain where the Jacobites meant to launch their first attack. The dukes of Atholl and Perth led the first part, travelling on the road to Peebles, from where they would progress through Moffat and Lockerbie to Carlisle. The prince and Murray led the second part, which left one day later, on 3 November, and took a route to the east of the others, progressing over the next few days through Lauder, Kelso and Jedburgh. From Kelso, a group of cavalry was sent out in a southeasterly direction to maintain the pretence that the army was intent on moving directly to Newcastle. It rejoined the main body of troops later on. From Jedburgh, Charles's division of the army turned southwest and headed towards the western extremity of the border with England. They crossed the Esk into England on 8 November at Gritmill Green. The next day, they met up with the division of the army that had taken the westerly route. Over the course of the journey, there had been a number of desertions, mostly from the prince's division, which consisted mostly of Highlanders. His entire force now numbered around 5000 men.

The army encamped for the night to the west of Carlisle, the prince finding lodgings in the village of Moorhouse. The next day, they advanced upon Carlisle and surrounded the town. A letter was sent in to the town demanding its surrender, but no surrender was given. News now came to the Jacobites that General Wade had left Newcastle and was marching with his army towards Carlisle. The prince determined to intercept him and leaving a small part of his army behind at Carlisle, advanced as far as Brampton. The following morning, scouts returned to the Jacobite army with the news that the rumour regarding General Wade's advance had been a hoax. Accordingly, the duke of Perth was sent back to Carlisle with a large division of the army to lay siege to Carlisle. The Jacobites spent a day building siege works around Carlisle, undeterred by the shots fired from the garrison within the town walls. The defenders of the town were not able to withstand the pressure of waiting for an attack for long. The next day, negotiations began for the surrender of Carlisle. Town and castle alike surrendered. The gates of the town were opened to the Jacobites. The members of the garrison who submitted were offered the chance of serving in the prince's army. All weapons and horses were seized for the Jacobite army. On 16 November, the Pretender was declared at the town cross.

Charles returned to Carlisle and spent five days there with his army. In many respects the capture of the town was a high point in the enterprise. It was their first victory in England and it had been won with hardly any bloodshed. It was bound to shake the morale of the army of George II. But the dissension among the leaders in the Jacobite army was getting worse. Tensions between Lord George Murray and the duke of Perth escalated after a dispute over who should have taken overall command of the siege and first Murray then Perth resigned their posts as lieutenant-generals. A petition from the army requested that Lord George should be given overall command and reinstated as lieutenant-general, and Perth eventually acquiesced.

Upon hearing of the siege of Carlisle, Wade had marched from Newcastle with all haste, with the intention of relieving the town. Unfortunately, only a few days into the journey, his army's progress was blocked by heavy snowfall. The adverse weather conditions, and the news that the Jacobites had already taken Carlisle, resolved him to go no further. He turned back for Newcastle.

CHAPTER THIRTY-FOUR

The Advance from Carlisle

The Jacobite leaders debated their next course of action. They could march on Newcastle and engage Wade's army in battle. An alternative plan was to leave Wade in Newcastle and march directly towards London through Lancashire, gathering support from the Lancashire Jacobites en route. This plan was risky, for there was no certainty that the hoped-for additional support would be forthcoming. Moreover, Jacobite spies had news of another large government force being mustered in the south, and moving northwards. The third alternative, which Murray would have preferred, was to move back north into Scotland to await the arrival of support from France. After some debate, it was decided that the prince's preferred option should be taken, to march south by the western route, via Preston and Worcester. The army moved out in two sections on 21 and 22 November. Murray led the first section, which consisted of most of the Lowland regiments and Elcho's horse. The prince led the second section; the Highlanders and the remaining cavalry. The first section reached Penrith on the first night, and in the morning advanced to Kendal, while the second, having moved out of Carlisle on the second day, reached Penrith. In this way the army progressed, one section following in the footsteps of the other, on to Lancaster, Garstang and then Preston.

The progress of the army was incredibly fast, given that it was winter. The prince's determination to maintain the morale of his men was commendable. Rather than travelling on horseback, he opted to march alongside his men, shrugging off the effects of fatigue and cold. The men had little to feed themselves with except the stores of oatmeal they carried in pouches around their waists. The loyalty, perseverance and strength of character of the men who marched with the prince must have heartened him greatly, but the journey was not without disappointment. Their progress might have been unopposed, but the support that the prince had been counting on from the English Jacobites was still not forthcoming. Recruits came to the army, but in tens rather than hundreds and on the whole, the reception that greeted the Jacobite army as it passed from place to place was never more than lukewarm.

At Preston, the whole army joined together once more. Murray's section arrived on 25 November, and Charles and his men arrived the following day. The Jacobites stayed long enough to gather much-needed money from the town, before marching out again on 28 November and marching to Wigan, where they spent one night. The next stop would be Manchester, where they expected to be able to recruit considerably more men than they had managed to gather so far. They entered Manchester on 29 November to find that a man called Dickson had been making strenuous efforts on the prince's behalf. Arriving in the town on his own the day before, he had risked his life by standing in the centre of town calling up able-bodied citizens to the Jacobite army. It was only after a crowd of angry Mancunians threatened to capture him that Jacobite supporters finally came to his aid. By the end of the day, the numbers had grown and Dickson found himself with a force of around 500 men, now called the Manchester Regiment. The prince's arrival bought in more recruits and, as at Preston, men were sent out to gather what monies they could to swell the army's treasury and find more horses for the conveyance of both men and supplies. On 1 December, the Jacobites were on the move once again, continuing their progress south by way of Stockport.

So far, progress had been rapid principally because it had been unopposed. But the fortunes of Charles's army would soon change. An encounter with government troops was looking increasingly likely, and in the near future. The Jacobites had reached Macclesfield when news came to them that the duke of Cumberland was moving north with his army and was already in Staffordshire, to the south of them. The decision was taken to continue in a southeasterly direction from Macclesfield and march to Derby, thereby avoiding Cumberland's army as it moved north.

In order to keep Cumberland safely to the west of the Jacobite army, efforts were made to ensure that the Hanoverian leader received false intelligence as to the Jacobite army's whereabouts. As a ruse to make Cumberland think that the Jacobites might be heading for Wales rather than London, Murray led a large proportion of the army out of Macclesfield in a short detour southwest to Congleton. Cumberland, hearing of Murray's movements and acting on the supposition that Murray's men were the advance guard of the entire army, moved his troops north to Stone, to the south of Murray's position, ready for an encounter. While Cumberland waited at Stone, Murray led his men from Congleton, passed to the east of Cumberland's position and joined up with Prince Charles and the rest of the army at Ashbourne. Charles's section of the army had reached Ashbourne by way of Leek, marching through the night for the second part of their journey. From Ashbourne an advance party was sent on to Derby to prepare for the arrival of the army, which came into the town in piecemeal fashion over the course of the day. The prince's father was duly proclaimed in the town centre and bonfires were lit in celebration that night.

It was 4 December. It was less than four months since the Jacobite standard had been unfurled at Glenfinnan, and a little more than five months since the prince had first set sail from France. In that time, the prince had seen his army grow from seven men to five thousand. He had taken control of the Scottish capital. And now, having reached a point further south than any previous invasion of England by Scots, he was less than 130 miles from the capital of England. In the years that have passed since the rebellion of 1745, there has been much criticism of the character of Charles, and his tactical approach to the rebellion. But the scale of the prince's achievement in getting as far as he did, his optimism and determination and his faith in the men who followed him can never be understated. It was a feat his father would certainly never have dared contemplate, far less attempt to accomplish.

CHAPTER THIRTY-FIVE

The Retreat Begins

The position of the Jacobite army in Derby was as follows. To the west of them was Cumberland's army of more than 8000 men, which had fallen back on Stafford. Wade's army had moved out of Newcastle, and was now closing in on them from the east. To the north of the city of London, the Jacobites had reports that a third, smaller Hanoverian army had been gathering on Finchley Common. The Jacobite men were tired from many days' marching in cold weather with meagre rations. Their numbers were good and morale was high, but their strength was lower than it might be. In addition to that, the Highlanders, accustomed to fighting in the high ground, rocky and rough terrain that characterised their homeland, were as yet untested in what must have seemed to them to have been an alien land. The army was isolated in its position in Derby – there was no certainty of help from any direction. And yet they were within one week's march of the capital city and the bright hope of victory.

The prince, ever the optimist and bold adventurer, was all for pressing on, beating Cumberland in the race to London and taking the capital by storm. His leaders did not agree. The clash of personalities between Lord George Murray and the prince had been a source of friction from the outset. Murray felt confident in his skills as a military tactician and assumed the right to advise the young, inexperienced and impetuous prince on military matters. Charles, on the other hand, resented Murray's advice and felt that Murray was questioning his authority. Up until this point in the enterprise, the prince had been able to have his way when it came to major decisions, in spite of Murray's expressed misgivings. Charles' persuasiveness and determination had kept the army on the move, while Murray's tactics and strategies had helped to keep it safe. This time it was clear that there was no way of talking Murray or any of the other leaders round. They were not willing to put the lives of their men or their prince at such risk when the odds were so heavily stacked against them. Charles had no choice. The decision was taken out of his hands. The army would turn back from Derby and head for Scotland.

An advance party had already been sent south to take Swarkstone Bridge across the River Trent. They had to be recalled. On 6 December, the army moved out of Derby.

Much has been made of the 'what-ifs' of the Jacobites' situation at this point, and some historians have argued that an advance on London might have succeeded. One of the main sources of worry for the Jacobite leaders, throughout the English part of the campaign, had been lack of support, either from England or from France. Now, it looked as if that support might be forthcoming. News of the arrival of the army on Derby had heartened many English Jacobites and there were signs that a significant number were preparing to rise in both England and Wales. In London, meanwhile, news of Charles's progress had been greeted with dismay in Whig circles and delight among Jacobite supporters. Anticipating the army's arrival in the capital in a matter of days, it is said that George II had made preparations to sail down the Thames to safety at the first sign of their approach. The demand for money from the Bank of England was such that it was threatened with closure. Meanwhile, Jacobite sympathisers were waiting to pledge their support for the prince the moment he arrived.

Now, at last, a significant response had also come from France. In the middle of October, Louis had formally recognised James Edwards Stewart's claim to the throne and had arranged for more than a thousand troops from the Irish Brigade, under the command of the exiled Lord John Drummond, to be sent to Scotland. Although vessels carrying approximately one third of the troops were captured by Royal Navy ships, the rest made it safely to the north east of Scotland, landing in the second half of November. In addition to this, plans had been put in place for a full-scale invasion in England. A considerable force was being assembled in Channel ports, ready to sail for ports in the southwest of England, to the great alarm of the English authorities. The force was on the point of departure when news reached France that the prince had abandoned the advance on London.

If the Jacobites had advanced on London, it is most likely that they would have got there before Cumberland. It is possible that they could have taken the capital. But could they have held it? The French fleet was still in France in the middle of December. Even if it had reached England safely, it might have been too late. Drummond's men in the northeast of Scotland were too far away to support the action in the south. And since the Young Pretender's army had crossed the border, the Jacobite hold on Scotland was weakening.

The possibilities are tantalising, but from the perspective of the leaders of the Jacobite army, the reality was not encouraging.

CHAPTER THIRTY-SIX

Back to the Border

Progress north was rapid, but grim, as the Jacobite army retraced its steps through Ashbourne, Leek, Macclesfield, and Manchester. After five days' marching, the dispirited troops arrived in Preston. Cumberland, having only been alerted to the Jacobites' withdrawal from Derby two days after the event, hurried to Macclesfield and tagged behind them, waiting for his chance. Charles was reluctant to hurry, believing that an engagement with the Hanoverians would relieve some of the ignominy of retreat, but Murray, aware that they were risking no simple encounter but the possibility of becoming hemmed in by Cumberland and Wade's forces together, urged the prince on with dogged persistence. The prince took the vanguard while Murray followed up in the rear. From Preston, to Lancaster, to Kendal, the army trudged on in the bleakest of winter weather conditions.

On the night of 17 December, the prince's section of the army had reached Penrith, but the rear was lagging some way behind, owing to difficulties moving the heaviest equipment. On 18 December, they had almost reached the village of Clifton when they caught sight of an advance party of Hanoverian troops. Without knowledge of the numbers they were likely to face, Murray settled upon taking up concealed defensive positions, behind walls and ditches either side of the road that ran through the village as night began to fall. When the first of the Hanoverians began to advance and spread out on either side of the road, Murray gave the order to attack. The Highlanders – Stewarts of Glengarry and Appin, and Cluny Macpherson's regiment – fell upon the Hanoverians with great vigour, sending them swiftly into retreat, back to the main body of their army. In the struggle, which was later to become known as the 'Skirmish of Clifton', forty men of the Hanoverian army were killed and five of the Highlanders lost their lives. It was the last Jacobite conflict on English soil.

Murray's rearguard caught up with the prince's portion of the army at Carlisle, where they spent the night of 19 December. Leaving a garrison at Carlisle to hold the city, they marched on to the border with Scotland at the River Esk. The crossing proved to be a hazardous and difficult exercise as the river was running high and fast with flood water after several days of bad weather, but it was achieved with minimal loss of life and by late afternoon, the army was on home territory once again.

Back in Carlisle, the garrison that had been left behind was far less fortunate. The day after the Jacobite army left, Cumberland arrived. In spite of relentless battering of the castle and town walls from Hanoverian canon, the garrison, which consisted of the Manchester regiment and 300 men from the Scottish regiments, held out for several days. On 30 December, they finally surrendered and the town gates were opened to Cumberland's men. Cumberland showed none of the leniency that Charles had displayed when the last garrison had surrendered to the Jacobite army. The Jacobites were all imprisoned and months later, after being brought to trial, many of them were executed and most of the rest transported to the colonies.

CHAPTER THIRTY-SEVEN

From the Borders to Falkirk

Since Charles's departure from Scotland, the government had been taking measures to regain its hold on the country. Almost as soon as Edinburgh was vacated by the Jacobite army, the city was re-taken. The castle at Stirling, which had remained in the hands of government troops, had received reinforcements. The town and the crossing of the Forth were well guarded. In the north, Inverness was now held by Whigs. Following the Jacobites' withdrawal from England, the duke of Cumberland was recalled to the south, where it was still thought likely that a French force might land. General Wade was left in command of troops in the north of England, while Lieutenant-General Hawley was ordered to take command of an army to lead into Scotland.

The Jacobite army was divided into two sections for the move northwards. Murray would lead one part through Ecclefechan, Moffat, and Hamilton while the prince led the rest through Annan, Dumfries, and Drumlanrig before moving on to Douglas. The two parts would converge on Glasgow, which, although it was a city unsympathetic to the Jacobite cause, was a less dangerous proposition than the capital. The prince's progress was less rapid than that of Murray. He spent a night in Annan, then another in Dumfries. At all times, the prince maintained an air of confidence, in spite of the withdrawal from England. In Dumfries, £2000 was levied from the people of the town and hundreds of pairs of shoes were ordered for the troops. The prince was comfortably accommodated in a house in town that was later to become the Commercial Inn. The threat of government forces following to the rear moved the army on the following day and they proceeded to Drumlanrig, seat of the duke of Queensberry. From Drumlanrig they moved on to Douglas, where the prince spent the night in Douglas Castle, and then to Hamilton. At Hamilton, the prince paused to enjoy a day's hunting before continuing his journey to Glasgow.

Glasgow had grown large and prosperous in recent years but its commercial wealth was not matched by strong defences. Murray's men entered the city on 25 December and the prince's men on 26 December. The reaction of the citizens was hostile and resentful, but no significant resistance was made to the occupation, except for the action of one rash individual who fired a shot at the prince in the Saltmarket, but missed. Charles found comfortable accommodation for himself in Shawfield House. He used the next few days to review his troops and to do what he could to restore their torn and bedraggled apparel. The city found itself obliged to provide the Jacobite army with 12,000 shirts, 6000 pairs of shoes and 6000 pairs of hose. Faced with the threat of the Highlanders ransacking and burning the whole town, the citizens complied, but not without complaint. In Glasgow, the prince also found the time to entertain.

Eight days later, the army left Glasgow. The break had been sorely needed. By the time they reached the city, the army was desperately tired. Many of the men had worn their shoes to nothing and were marching with bare feet. They had been short of clothing, arms and food. The money levied from Glasgow and surrounding towns was not only welcome, but desperately needed and the clothing so grudgingly provided by the Glaswegians was essential. The departure from the city on 3 January saw the army much refreshed and stronger after its stay.

Once again, they marched out in two sections. Charles led his men to Kilsyth, while Murray proceeded with his to Cumbernauld. After a night at Kilsyth, Charles moved on to Bannockburn, where he was the guest of Sir Hugh Paterson at Bannockburn House. The army stayed at Bannockburn for a few days and during this time, they were joined by the forces brought from France by Lord John Drummond and a considerable body of men under the command of John Lewis of Gordon. The men raised by Gordon himself consisted of two battalions from Aberdeenshire. These had been reinforced in Perth, thanks to the efforts of Lord Strathallan, who had assembled several hundred Frasers, 400 Mackintoshes, members of the Mackenzie clan and Clanranald Macdonalds and others. In total, the additions to the Jacobite army amounted to around 4000 men. From their base at Bannockburn, the Jacobites moved in on Stirling. The town surrendered fairly quickly on 6 January but the castle held out.

The value of taking Stirling and embarking on a siege at this point in the campaign was doubtful. Edinburgh was better defended than it had been before, but if the Jacobite army had been quick off the mark from Glasgow, there might have still been the opportunity to seize it for the Pretender before Hawley arrived with his force from the south. As it was, the Jacobites wasted valuable days laying siege to the castle in Stirling while Hawley arrived in the capital, and assembled his army. At Edinburgh, the force that Hawley had brought with him from England was swelled by the Glasgow and Paisley militia, who had fled to the capital as the Jacobite army approached Glasgow. The dragoons, which had so badly let down the Hanoverian side when Charles made his first entrance into Edinburgh and again at Preston, were reinforced by Cobham's dragoons and a small company called the Yorkshire Blues. Hawley's army numbered in total around 8000 men.

On 13 January, Hawley sent an advance body of men under Major-General Huske from Edinburgh to Linlithgow. Lord George Murray, who had taken a party of Jacobite Highlanders from Stirling towards Linlithgow, heard of their approach and retired back to Falkirk, then to Bannockburn. It was now clear that an encounter with the Hanoverian army was imminent and the Jacobite army began preparations.

On 16 January, Hawley moved out of Edinburgh with the remainder of his army and set up camp to the northwest of Falkirk. The next day, his army was further increased by the arrival of Lieutenant–Colonel John Campbell, with approximately 1000 clansmen. Hawley's intention was to drive the Jacobites from Stirling and relieve the siege of the castle. He did not anticipate that the Jacobites would draw him into battle before his army reached

Stirling. But while the Hanoverian army was moving towards Falkirk, Charles was preparing for battle. On 15 January, his army moved approximately two miles east from Bannockburn and set up an encampment on Plean Moor.

Although situated more than five miles apart, the lights from the fires of the two armies were visible to one another at night across the level ground that stretched between them.

Hawley's attitude remained confident and relaxed. Believing that the Jacobites would wait where they were, he spent the night of 16 January being entertained at Callendar House in Falkirk by the Countess of Kilmarnock, apparently oblivious to the fact that the Countess's husband was serving in the Jacobite army. The next morning, he was back there again, taking breakfast. He remained there, completely relaxed, for the remainder of the morning.

The Jacobite commanders were not as willing to wait as Hawley had anticipated. On the morning of 17 January, a war council was held and the leaders agreed that their best move was to take the Hanoverian army with a surprise offensive. As a decoy, Drummond was sent with a body of cavalry along the road which approached Falkirk from the north. Meanwhile, the main body of the Jacobite army moved southwest from Plean Moor, towards the River Carron, fording it at the Steps of Dunipace and moving swiftly down and round towards Falkirk Muir, approaching it from the southwest.

The Hanoverians grew alarmed when they saw the Jacobite army was on the move, but Hawley was slow to react. The Jacobites had reached the River Carron when the Hanoverian general was finally convinced of the imminent danger. Hastily taking leave of his hostess, he hurried from Callander House to join his army who were rallying for action. The race was now on to reach the top of the hill, known as Falkirk Muir.

The weather, which had been relatively calm and clear during the morning, now turned severe. A strong southwesterly wind began to blow, accompanied by heavy rain. As the Jacobites headed towards the hill in two orderly columns, the wind was at their backs, whilst the Hanoverians struggled against the cold rain driving into their faces. The dragoons were sent ahead in front of the foot soldiers of Hawley's army, in the hope that they would gain possession of the highest ground before the Jacobites, but they were not fast enough. As they rode uphill, the Jacobites were already assembling at the top in two lines, facing west. The Hanoverian army assembled to face them at fairly close proximity on a lower part of the high ground. Between the larger part of both armies, running from north to south, stretched a gorge, widening towards the bottom of the hill. The armies were roughly equal in size – approximately 8000 men in each. It was almost four o'clock in the afternoon and it would soon be dark.

The dragoons, positioned on the left of the Hanoverian lines, were ordered to move forward. They advanced towards the Highlanders on the right wing of the Jacobite army, hoping to draw their fire before they moved in for a full attack. Lord George Murray was in command of the right wing, which was composed mostly of Macdonalds. With considerable difficulty, he held his men in check until the dragoons were close enough for gunfire to be effective, then gave the command for them to fire. The first shots from the Highland muskets cut into the dragoons with deadly effect. A large number of the surviving dragoons turned away at once and tried to flee, leaving the rest of the men to continue with the advance unsupported. They charged into the ranks of the Macdonalds, and several of the Highlanders in the front line were flung to the ground by the impact of the charge. The fallen men continued to fight ferociously, slashing at the horses' bellies with their dirks to bring them down. Macdonald of Clanranald found himself pinned to the ground by a fallen horse. He lay helpless for some moments, watching while one of his fellow clansmen struggled violently in a fight to the death with one of the dragoons. The Highlander emerged victorious and pulled his chief clear, enabling him to carry on fighting.

The retreat of the dragoons that had been driven back by the first onslaught of fire, meanwhile, was far from orderly and was causing havoc in the infantry lines of the Hanoverian army. The Macdonalds, spurred on by their success in repelling the horsemen, now charged forward into left of the infantry, ignoring Murray's command to hold back.

The left wing of the Jacobites was in a more vulnerable position. They had taken longer than the right to assemble in fighting order and were now faced by an attack from the Hanoverian infantry opposite them, supported by another body of cavalry. Almost as soon as the English horse advanced into the front line of Highlanders, the Highland second line came forward *en masse* in support, in spite of musket fire being poured upon them from the extreme right of the Hanoverian army, which had as yet not entered the battle. The force of the full-frontal Highland attack was devastating. With the rain driving into their faces and wetting their muskets and rendering them useless, the Hanoverian infantry found themselves helpless in the face of such opposition. The battle was over in less than half an hour. Only the extreme right wing of the English army were spared the devastation that was wreaked upon their comrades. They withdrew to Falkirk in relatively good order, while the bulk of the other survivors retreated in more chaotic fashion.

It was undoubtedly a substantial victory for the prince's army. Hanoverian casualties amounted to several hundred dead or wounded and several hundred more were taken prisoner. In contrast, the Jacobite casualties were less than 200, and less than 40 of them dead. But the victory was incomplete. Hawley and a good number of his men had been able to retreat without pursuit. Murray led his troops into Falkirk that night, but the Hanoverians had already gone and were soon safely in Linlithgow. No attempt was made to catch up with them and destroy them. The failure to follow up the battle and finish off Hawley's force was criticised by many Jacobite leaders as a major tactical error. Had Hawley's army been completely crushed, the way would have been open to take Edinburgh back for the Pretender. As it was, the Hanoverian army had been stalled, but not stopped, and in real terms, the Jacobite cause was no further forward.

Chapter Thirty-Eight

From Falkirk to Inverness

On the day after the battle of Falkirk, the Jacobites set about gathering what spoils they could and burying their dead. People from the districts around the town were brought to the site of the battle to dig a great pit, in which the bodies, terribly mutilated by cuts from broadswords and daggers, were interred. Charles returned to Bannockburn House, while Lord George Murray remained with a body of men in Falkirk. The rest of the prince's army resumed the siege of Stirling Castle. Morale in the Jacobite ranks was low, in spite of their recent victory, and spirits sank further with the prospect of another period of relative inactivity, waiting in vain for the garrison in Stirling Castle to submit. As January drew to a close, Charles's army was significantly reduced by desertions.

Hawley, meanwhile, had returned to the capital, humiliated by the defeat of his army and determined not to accept any of the blame. Four of his officers were hanged on his orders for cowardice. Several more men were whipped. His efforts at covering up his failure were in vain, however, for as soon as news of the defeat at Falkirk was carried to the court in London, the duke of Cumberland was summoned and ordered to resume command of the Hanoverian army in Scotland. After his failure to stop the prince's army in England, Cumberland was eager for another chance to prove his military prowess and anxious for revenge upon the Jacobites. He set off for the Scottish capital at once. By the end of January, he had taken command and was ensconced in Holyrood House, holding councils with General Hawley and General Huske and assessing his troops and arms. Before his arrival, the Hanoverian army had been further reinforced by troops from northern England and the Continent. In addition to these troops, a number of officers who had been captured by the Jacobites at Preston and then released upon their word not to fight against the Stewarts for the period of a year, were brought to Edinburgh and persuaded to rejoin their regiments in the Hanoverian army.

In the Jacobite camp, things were going from bad to worse. The siege was proving as fruitless as ever and several men had lost their lives in the effort. All active attempts at taking the castle were abandoned. The size of the army was diminishing daily as more and more Highlanders slipped away to return to their homes. The Jacobite army was now considerably smaller than the force that Cumberland had under his command. The prince was still optimistic that his men could resume the offensive and perhaps even return to England to take up the campaign there once more, but the leaders of his army were not of the same opinion. When news reached the Jacobite camp of Cumberland's arrival in Edinburgh, the prince called his leaders to council, hoping for a plan of battle to be agreed upon. To his dismay, his leaders presented a united front against this idea. They were all of the same opinion. The Jacobite army should withdraw to the Highlands. The withdrawal was not proposed as a retreat, but a tactical move, to give the army time in the winter months to increase again to full strength. Deserters could be re-recruited and hopefully, more troops from France would arrive. The forts in the north held by Hanoverian troops could be captured and by spring, the army would be stronger and better placed to take on Cumberland. The prince was devastated, but his attempts to persuade the chiefs to stay and fight were in vain. On 31 January, Cumberland moved out of Edinburgh at the head of his army. On the same day, Lord George Murray withdrew his troops from Falkirk to Bannockburn to join the rest of the army.

The Jacobites moved out of Stirling on 1 February in haste. Large numbers of the rank and file, hearing that a withdrawal was about to take place, began to move out of the town before the order had been given, which infuriated Murray. In view of the difficult journey that lay ahead, the decision was taken to leave much of the heavier artillery and equipment behind. The cannon were disabled. The rest was destroyed or thrown into the river.

After a night at Dunblane and Doune, the Jacobite army moved on to Perth and Crieff. At Crieff, after bitter debate between Charles and Lord George Murray, it was eventually decided that the army should be split in two for the march north. Charles would lead one body of men, consisting mostly of Highlanders, along Wade's road through the Highlands from Aberfeldy to Inverness. Lord George Murray would lead the Lowland regiments and the artillery eastwards, and travel north along the coastal roads through Angus and Aberdeenshire, meeting with Charles's detachment at Inverness.

At this stage, it was already clear that the Jacobite army had one distinct advantage over Cumberland's great force. The Jacobite army, having a large proportion of men who were used to rapid marching in difficult conditions, and having unburdened them-selves of the most cumbersome of their baggage (more was left behind at Perth), was much more manoeuvrable than Cumberland's army. While the Jacobite army progressed relatively rapidly, Cumberland was forced to stall for a day at Stirling while the bridge over the river, which had been destroyed by Hanoverian troops ear-lier in the rebellion, was repaired in order to allow passage for his artillery. When Cumberland began the pursuit of the Jacobite army he was barely one day behind them. By the time he reached Perth on 6 February, their lead had stretched considerably. The eastern contingent were now between Montrose and Aberdeen, whilst the part of the Jacobite army heading through the Highlands was already well past Blair on the road to Inverness.

At Perth, realising that the poor weather would further hamper progress, Cumberland stropped for a few days to gather supplies and reconsider his tactics. During this time, he received news of the landing of the prince of Hesse on the shores of the Forth at Leith with 5000 auxiliary troops from Europe. He travelled back to Edinburgh to greet the new arrivals and returned to Perth with them following. On 20 February, he left Perth at the head of his army and after a week's travel, reached Aberdeen. He used the newly arrived Hessian troops to hold open lines of communication from Perth to the north. The country was still in the grip of winter, and Cumberland decided at this point that the wisest course of action would be to stop in Aberdeen for a few weeks. Waiting until the weather improved would afford him time to rest his men, increase his army to full strength and train them for a decisive conflict in the spring.

February saw a number of minor victories for the Jacobite forces. An advance party of men from Charles's contingent captured Ruthven Barracks in the second week of February, two or three days before the prince arrived. The commander of the barracks gave up without a struggle. The prince spent two nights with his contingent at Ruthven before they moved on, towards Inverness. On 15 February, the prince slept at Inverlaidnan House and, on 16 February, he moved to Moy Hall, seat of the laird of Mackintosh, less than ten miles to the southeast of Inverness. The laird was a Whig and was away on service in the government army, but his wife, Lady Anne Mackintosh, was a staunch Jacobite and had raised the clan members to fight for the prince, thereby earning herself the nickname 'Colonel Anne'. While Charles was at Moy, enjoying the generous hospitality of the 'colonel', an incident took place that might have spelled a more sudden end for Jacobite hopes had it not been for the quick thinking and action of a few loyal supporters.

Lord Loudon of Inverness, who was in charge of the government troops in the town, had heard of the prince's whereabouts and decided to take the opportunity to make a surprise attack on Moy and capture the prince. Leaving enough of his men behind to guard Inverness, he assembled a force of approximately 1500 and set out in the dead of night towards Moy. Fortunately for the prince, the laird's mother, the dowager Lady Mackintosh, who was staying in Inverness, was alerted to the fact that Loudon was preparing his men for some sort of action and realised what was afoot. She sent a young messenger, Lachlan Mackintosh, to overtake Loudon's men before they reached Moy and give warning to the prince. The boy was hard-pressed to succeed in his mission without being found

out, but after taking a shortcut over marsh and moor land in the
second part of his journey, managed to reach Moy Hall before
Loudon's men and give warning to the prince's bodyguard, who
woke the prince. Charles slipped away from Moy Hall just after five
in the morning and joined the men of Lochiel, who were positioned about a mile away on the shore of Loch Moy.

Charles and Lochiel were ready to stand their ground and fight,
but by a combination of good fortune and cunning, they were
spared the effort. As a precautionary measure, Lady Mackintosh
had sent a group of five men out the evening before to keep a night
watch, a couple of miles away on the road from Inverness to Moy.
The leader of the group was a man called Fraser, a blacksmith. As
soon as Fraser became aware of the approach of Loudon's men
along the road, he ordered the rest of the men in the group to
spread themselves out at various points on either side of the road
while he faced in the direction from which Loudon's men were
coming. As the vanguard of Loudon's company drew near, Fraser
fired his musket, killing the piper. The others in the group fired
from their positions and Fraser gave a great shout, calling the
advance to an invisible horde of Camerons and Macdonalds. This
war-cry, combined with the scattered gunfire, was enough to convince the front ranks of Loudon's men that they were in the midst
of the main body of the Jacobite army and at once, they turned tail
and fled, causing chaos as they rushed in a panic back through the
ranks behind them. As soon as they could gather their wits, the rest
of Loudon's men joined in the flight back to Inverness. The incident was to become known as 'the Rout of Moy'.

Having been informed of the brave blacksmith's triumph, the
prince returned to Moy Hall for another night. The next day, after
assembling his army, he led them on to Inverness. They entered the
town unopposed. Loudon and his men were retreating from
Inverness towards the crossing to the Black Isle at Kessock as the
Jacobites advanced into the town. Only Fort George held out
against the prince's army, but after a siege of two days, this too was
surrendered on 20 February. The Jacobites, having plundered it of
a good supply of arms, ammunition and food, then destroyed it.

At Inverness, the Jacobite army was assembled in its entirety once again when Lord George Murray's contingent arrived, a day after Charles's entrance into the town. A party of Jacobites led by the earl of Cromarty set off in pursuit of Loudon's regiment, but in spite of dogging their tracks into Ross-shire, failed to catch up with them.

From their base in Inverness, sections of the Jacobite army engaged in a number of minor conflicts, which did much to improve morale, but in reality did little substantially to improve their position. At the end of February, 300 men were sent under the command of Brigadier Stapleton to capture Fort Augustus. They captured the barracks and laid siege to the fort. Fortune played a hand in bringing the siege to a conclusion. A shell fired into the gunpowder store only two days after the siege began caused a large explosion and the garrison were forced to concede defeat. The same party of Jacobites then advanced to Fort William, where, reinforced by a body of Camerons, Macdonalds and Stewarts under the command of Lochiel, they embarked upon another siege. Unfortunately, there were difficulties in transporting the artillery that was needed to bombard the fort and it did not arrive until the third week in March. The siege was still underway when the troops were recalled at the beginning of April in anticipation of Cumberland's advance towards Inverness, and it had to be abandoned.

The pursuit of Loudon's troops into Ross-shire was taken up by Lord George Murray, who caught up with the earl of Cromarty's detachment at Dingwall. Loudon's men, and with them Duncan Forbes of Culloden, the president of the court of session and the government's chief representative in the Highlands, had already crossed the Dornoch Firth and were in Sutherland. The difficulty now for the Jacobites was how to launch an attack from this position. If the Jacobites moved around the head of the Dornoch Firth, their advance would be too slow. Loudon would be forewarned of their approach and, having boats at his disposal, would be able to return across the water into Easter Ross.

Murray did not wait for the conclusion of the action. He withdrew the troops to Dingwall, then handed over command to the duke of Perth and headed back to Inverness. There, he ordered the procurement of a number of fishing boats, sufficient to carry 800 of the men under the duke of Perth's command, across the Dornoch Firth from Tain. The vessels successfully evaded government ships blockading the entrance to the Moray Firth, thanks to a deep fog, and moved round the coast to Tain, where a large contingent of the duke of Perth's men, having moved back north from Dingwall, were waiting to be hastily embarked. The rest of his men moved round the head of the firth, to cut off the enemy's escape in that direction. The crossing of the Dornoch Firth was achieved and the force divided into two, the first division heading for Dornoch, where Loudon was staying and the second, to Overskibo, where Duncan Forbes of Culloden was in residence. The government troops under Forbes and Loudon were already demoralised and considerably reduced in numbers by desertion. When the Jacobite troops appeared, few of them showed any willingness to stand and fight. Forbes and Loudon, unfortunately, were not captured. They managed to make good their escape and eventually found safe passage, with a few hundred of their men, to Skye. The rest of their troops were dispersed. It was a successful episode for the Jacobites, but in retrospect, it is clear that the success was limited and it was achieved at the expense of considerable manpower, effort and time.

The prince was taken ill with pneumonia during this time and forced to remain inactive whilst Lord George Murray took the lead in the Jacobites' guerilla warfare. After leaving the duke of Perth to command the enterprise in Easter Ross and Sutherland, Murray took the initiative again, this time in Speyside and Atholl, where detachments of Cumberland's men had occupied several properties, most of which belonged to Jacobites. Murray's own family seat, Blair Castle, was occupied by a garrison under the command of Sir Andrew Agnew. In the middle of March, Murray set out from Inverness with a body of approximately 700 men. In Speyside, his men surrounded Castle Grant and persuaded its occupants, Lord Nairne's regiment, to surrender without any difficulty. Murray then moved southwest to Dalnaspidal, a few miles south of Dalwhinnie. He divided his force into several smaller groups and sent them on their separate ways to take the detachments at various government outposts in surprise night attacks. Bun-Rannoch, the house of Kynnachin, the house of Lude, the house of Faskally and the Inn of Blair in the village of Blair Atholl were among the places targeted. The assaults were carried out swiftly and efficiently. Thirty properties were successfully attacked and more than 200 prisoners were taken. Resistance was minimal and no Jacobite blood was shed. Only the attack on the Inn of Blair was unsuccessful. The occupants managed to make good their escape and fled to Blair Castle, to give warning to Sir Andrew Agnew of what was happening.

Murray had arranged for his men to rendezvous after their work was done at the Bridge of Bruar, about two miles northwest of Blair Castle. At daybreak, Murray was waiting with a party of only 24 men at the Bridge of Bruar when he was told that Agnew was approaching with several hundred men. Retreat or flight would mean leaving the other raiding-parties open to attack as they returned to Bruar. Murray's alternative was daring and clever. He ordered his men to take cover behind a large turf wall in a field close to the bridge, and to spread themselves out as wide as possible. At the approach of Agnew's men, the pipers in the group began playing rousing music. Regimental colours were flown at intervals along the wall, and the Highlanders raised their broadswords to catch the light of the early morning sun. The flags, the noise and the bright flashes of light reflected from the swords served to convince Agnew's men that they had come upon a force of considerable size. They decided that retreat was the wisest option. They turned and headed back to safety behind the walls of Blair Castle.

As soon as Murray had reassembled his troops, he embarked upon a siege of Blair Castle. Unfortunately, without heavy artillery to bombard the castle, Murray was hard-pressed to make the siege successful. His men contained the occupants in the castle for two weeks, hoping to starve the garrison into surrender. At the beginning of April, hearing that a force of Hessian troops was coming from

Perth to relieve the siege, and unable to get the reinforcements he needed to fight them, Murray was forced to withdraw to the north again.

In the second half of March, another small victory was won by Jacobite forces in Speyside. Lord John Drummond was in command of a Jacobite outpost at Fochabers. Detachments of his men were posted at Cullen, ten miles to the northeast on the coast, and near Huntly in Strathbogie, to the southeast. Their placements were undisturbed by government troops until the middle of March, when, in preparation for his advance into Speyside, Cumberland began sending troops out from Aberdeen towards the Spey, to deal with Jacobite opposition to his progress. A large body of men under the command of General Bland was dispatched from Aberdeen in the middle of March with orders to deal with the detachment at Strathbogie. Fortunately, the Jacobites at Strathbogie were warned of Bland's approach and effected a hasty retreat, pursued by Bland's cavalry, to Fochabers. Most of the Jacobite force at Fochabers was stationed on the eastern side of the River Spey. Now they all withdrew to the western side.

Having secured Strathbogie for the Hanoverians, Bland sent a detachment of 100 of his men, mostly Campbells, to occupy the village of Keith, approximately five miles southeast of Fochabers. With Drummond's men now at the other side of the Spey, it is likely that the little detachment felt relatively secure in their placement. Drummond sent patrols across the river to Fochabers each day, but they never advanced as far as Keith and always returned before nightfall. On the night of 20 March, however, the Hanoverians at Keith were taken by surprise. Some time after the day patrol had returned across the river, a company of 50 men under the command of Captain Robert Stewart, and a number of French troops commanded by Major Nicholas Glasgow, left the Jacobite camp under cover of darkness and crossed the Spey. They made a stealthy advance to Keith and surrounded it without being detected. After seizing the guard, they entered the village and overpowered the occupying troops after a brief but bloody struggle. Seventy prisoners were taken and nine men killed. Jacobite casualties were light in comparison, with only one fatality.

The efficiency of the operation cannot be denied, and it undoubtedly heartened the Jacobites. Nonetheless, having lost their positions to the east of the Spey, they were now very much on the defensive against Cumberland's army.

CHAPTER THIRTY-NINE

Disappointments

When the Jacobites embarked on the withdrawal from Stirling, hopes were high that help would be forthcoming from the continent, in the form of money, arms, ammunition, and men. In February, four ships sailed from France with more than 500 men and horses to strengthen the Jacobite forces. On the crossing, they were intercepted by British ships and two of them were captured. Less than a quarter of the men reached Scotland, landing at Aberdeen in the third week in February. This was not to be the only blow for the Jacobites.

In March, the arrival of the *Prince Charles* from France was anxiously awaited. This vessel, originally named the *Hazard,* had been captured from the Hanoverians in November, whilst she was in Montrose Harbour. After her capture, the Jacobites renamed her and put her into service as a supply ship, to bring over provisions and finance from France. The journey was inevitably fraught with danger as government ships were constantly patrolling the British coast. Her expected arrival now was particularly crucial to the Jacobites, as the long winter had left them desperately short of money, and shortages were making it increasingly difficult for Charles to keep his army together. The *Prince Charles* was approaching the northeast Scottish coast in the last week of March, carrying more than £12,000 in gold along with supplies of arms, ammunition and some French soldiers, when she came under attack from an English man-of-war. In a running battle, the *Prince Charles* was driven round the northern tip of Scotland and forced to make a landing on the west side of the Kyle of Tongue. More than 30 men had been killed in the battle. The rest made it ashore with the treasure, but, the morning after they landed, they were attacked by a force of government soldiers under the command of Lord Reay. The men were taken capture and the arms and money seized. It was a considerable loss for the Jacobites.

CHAPTER FORTY

The Duke of Cumberland Advances

Whilst the Jacobite army was finding itself increasingly short of money and vital supplies, the duke of Cumberland was having no such problems. His army was kept well supplied by sea. At the beginning of April, a large number of ships carrying weapons, ammunition and other stores arrived in Aberdeen, in preparation for Cumberland's planned advance across the River Spey. The worst of the winter weather was now past and the Spey, which had been running high with the water from the melting snows, had receded to a point where it was fordable in a number of places. The Hanoverian army was fit and well trained for the forthcoming encounter. The time had come for Cumberland to make his move.

On 8 April, Cumberland left Aberdeen with the troops that had been stationed there and moved to Old Meldrum, where he joined the detachments under the command of Brigadier Mordaunt. After a night at Old Meldrum, he moved on to Banff. The whole army – more the 9000 men – was assembled around the villages on the northeast coast by 11 April. On 12 April, the advance to the Spey was underway. The duke divided his troops into three to make the crossing of the river at three fords a little way to the north (down-river) of Fochabers. The crossing was difficult, for the Spey is, at the best of times, a swift-flowing river and its waters notoriously treacherous. Nonetheless, the army crossed quite rapidly, waist-deep in water, with the loss of only one soldier and four women. On the other side of the river, Lord John Drummond and his brother, the duke of Perth, had little more than 2000 men to oppose the crossing. Their decision not to offer resistance to Cumberland's advance has been criticised, but the odds against their success, had they tried, were probably too great – 2000 was a number that was at once too small and too large. It was too small a number to take on the might of Cumberland's entire army, and it was too large a number to risk losing in the attempt. The rest of the Jacobite army were as yet unaware of Cumberland's advance, and were scattered in various places. They would not be in a position to come to their aid.

As Cumberland advanced through Elgin, Forres, and Nairn, Drummond and his brother retreated towards Inverness with their men. News had by now reached the prince that Cumberland was on the move, and the information was greeted with a mixed reaction. On the one hand, the men that were still in Inverness were eager to get the opportunity, at last, to do battle with Cumberland. On the other hand, the army was already suffering considerably from the hardships enforced upon them by lack of finance. They had not been paid in money for some weeks now and their diet was extremely restricted, consisting largely of oatmeal, which was given to them in place of wages. Morale was low, the men's strength was reduced by hunger and their numbers had been reduced by desertions.

Relations between the prince and Murray, who had returned from the fruitless siege of Blair Castle, were at breaking point. The prince's distrust of Murray had become so strong that he was now unwilling to listen to anything that he said to him, in spite of his talents in military matters. There was now no question that they would have to engage in battle. Cumberland's army was now very close at hand, encamped at Nairn. The debate now hinged on choosing a sight that was most favourable to the Highland army's particular style of fighting, and which would disadvantage the Hanoverians, with their larger numbers of mounted soldiers, to the greatest extent. Charles turned to John o' Sullivan, one of the seven men who had accompanied him from France, for advice, disregarding the fact that Murray was better placed to choose the most favourable site, given his knowledge of the terrain and his experience of fighting with Highland forces.

The site chosen by O'Sullivan was Drumossie Moor, close to Culloden House. It was a large stretch of level heath land approximately two miles east of Inverness. In Murray's opinion, the site was too open. Cumberland's artillery would have a clear view and unobstructed range for their cannons, placing the Highland troops in a very vulnerable position and preventing them from making an effective charge. Apart from an area of boggy ground to the north of the site, the ground was perfectly suited for cavalry, which gave Cumberland's army a further advantage. The site preferred by Murray lay on the other side of the River Nairn. The ground was rough, uneven, and boggy. The Highlanders would be better protected from cannon-fire and the bogginess of the terrain would make an effective cavalry charge against them difficult, if not impossible. The objection laid against Murray's choice of battle-ground lay in its position, which offered Cumberland's army the chance of bypassing them and taking Inverness.

On the afternoon of 15 April, against Murray's wishes, the Highland forces were moved onto Drumossie Moor. Owing to shortages of food, many men had wandered off in search of provisions in neighbouring districts and the assembled army was far below strength. In the Hanoverian camp at Nairn, meanwhile, the duke of Cumberland was in expansive mood. It was his birthday, and in celebration of the event, he had awarded his army a night's rest and recuperation, fortified with quantities of food and drink. Late in the afternoon, the Jacobite leaders, knowing that a full-scale battle on the moor meant putting their men at great risk, agreed that they should take the chance to launch a surprise night attack on Cumberland's men in their encampment.

Assembling the Jacobite troops proved to be a difficult task. Almost a third of them were absent from the main body of the army, searching for food. Officers were sent out to bring them back by whatever means possible, but many, desperate with hunger, could not be persuaded to return, even when they were threatened with execution. It was therefore a considerably reduced force that set off that evening. They went in two divisions. Murray led the first part of the army and Charles, the second. In order that their approach would be undetected, none of the rank and file was told of their destination. The route that they took avoided the main route to Nairn. It was a very dark night and the ground they were traversing was rough and marshy. They could not light torches to help them see their way. The darkness and difficult terrain made progress painfully slow and the men's hunger and fatigue exacerbated the problem. Lord George Murray's detachment, which was smaller than the prince's, made faster progress. Soon the prince's detachment was hopelessly far behind. When Murray's detachment was within three miles of Cumberland's camp, he stopped. It was clear that it would take a long time for the prince's men to catch up. Meanwhile, they still had some distance to travel to reach their objective and it seemed unlikely that they would get there before daybreak. In light of this, Murray and his attendant officers took the decision to turn back. When Charles received the news that Murray's column was already on its way back, his initial reaction was one of fury. However, at length he was persuaded of the wisdom of Murray's decision and determined instead that his men should make the best of a battle at Culloden.

If the march out had been difficult, the march back was even worse. The men were almost dropping with exhaustion and in spite of the fact that they now made their way by public road rather than cross-country, their progress was still painfully slow. It was after six o'clock in the morning when the first of them reached their original position. Some lay down to get what sleep they could on the open moor. Others, frantic with hunger, resumed their relentless search for food.

CHAPTER FORTY-ONE

The Battle of Culloden, 16 April 1746

The Jacobites had little time for sleep. At eleven o'clock in the morning on 16 April, the first of Cumberland's army appeared on the eastern horizon across at the far side of the moor. The prince, who had been alerted of Cumberland's approach, returned to the field from Culloden House and called his men to battle. When all that could be assembled were hastily brought together, he had little more than 5000 men under his command. However willing these men might be, they were in poor condition for fighting – hungry, physically exhausted and sleep-deprived. The army they faced, in comparison, was fresh and well fed and armed, vastly superior in artillery, cavalry and numbers. The weather, which had been so favourable to the Jacobites some months ago at the battle of Falkirk, now turned against them. Rain and sleet, backed by a strong easterly wind, was driving into their faces, stinging their eyes and making it difficult to see.

The Jacobites were drawn up in two lines ready for the battle. The Highlanders stood in the front line, with the men of Atholl on the right wing, and next to them the Camerons. Beside the Camerons were the Stewarts of Appin, then the Frasers. The Mackintoshes were in the centre of the front line, next to Farquharsons, the Macleans, and the Maclachlans. John Roy Stewart's regiment, and the Macdonalds of Clanranald, Keppoch, and Glengarry stood to the left of them. Lord George Murray was in command of the right wing, with Lord John Drummond on the left. The second line had fewer men – approximately 2000 – and was composed of the Lowland regiments, the Irish, and the French. Lord Ogilvie's regiment was on the right, and next to that, Lord Lewis Gordon's men. Glenbucket and the duke of Perth held the centre, with the Irish and French on the left. Charles, with a small company of life-guards, was positioned on a slight rise slightly to the rear of the right wing. Twelve cannon were distributed evenly between the fronts of the right and left wings and centre. The horse – sadly few in number compared to Cumberland's cavalry of more than 1000 – were posi-tioned behind the second line.

Cumberland's infantry were drawn up in three lines, with eight-een cannon distributed along the first line. The first line contained the most men and stretched the widest, with the second and third progressively smaller. The lines were spaced well apart from one another, to avoid the first falling back on the second and causing con-fusion if the Highlanders charged. The battalions of the second line were placed, like bricks in a wall, to cover the spaces between the battalions in the first. The third line was similarly placed. The earl of Albemarle took command of the front line. General Huske com-manded the second line, and Brigadier Mordaunt the third. Cumberland had used the time in Aberdeen to train his infantry well to deal with the terrible broadswords of the Highlanders they faced. Instead of thrusting their bayonets into the man directly opposite them, they were taught to aim for the man diagonally to their right. As the Highlander raised his right hand, holding his sword, the bay-onet could be thrust in under his arm, delivering a lethal blow.

The Hanoverian army advanced to within 500 yards of the Jacobite lines, while the Jacobites still worked to get the stragglers into battle order. When the Hanoverian cannon became stuck in a patch of boggy ground, it seemed as if there might be a chance to attack them there and then, but Murray would not consider making a move until his army was completely organised. The two armies remained at this distance and manoeuvred from side to side, each trying to outflank each other before battle commenced. Eventually, they settled in almost direct opposition to one another, with Cumberland's forces outflanking the Jacobites on both sides.

It was at about one o'clock in the afternoon when battle finally commenced with artillery fire from the Jacobites' side.

Unfortunately, their cannon were neither sufficient in numbers nor strong enough to make any impact. The Hanoverians began returning fire almost immediately and with deadly effect. The Hanoverian cannons pounded the Jacobite lines. To his great pleasure, Cumberland could see the Jacobite lines thinning out considerably. As men began to fall around them, the Highland troops grew increasingly restless and enraged, but their leaders still would not give the command to attack, perhaps wanting to wait until the Hanoverians moved closer, to improve their chances of an effective charge. Unfortunately, the Hanoverian commander had already seen for himself that there was no need for his men to advance at this point. The cannon were proving devastatingly effective, without placing the lives of any of his men in danger. For almost half an hour the cannonade continued, steady and relentless, and still the Highlanders were forced to remain immobile.

It is not entirely clear why it was not the prince who gave the order to charge when it was eventually given. It may be that he did give the order, but it was not passed on by his messenger. In the event, it was Lord George Murray who ordered the men to attack, without knowledge of whether the prince wished it or not.

As soon as the order had been given, the Mackintosh clan, in the centre of the front line, charged headlong into the fog of cannon-smoke ahead. The rest of the Highlanders in the centre and on the right swiftly followed, and Lord George Murray went with them. The larger part of the Jacobite front line was now engaged. Only the left wing, which consisted of different branches of the Macdonald clan, was slow to react. Some say that this was because the Macdonalds, who traditionally were positioned on the right wing of the army, were displeased that the men of the Atholl Brigade had taken their place on this occasion.

To the right of the Jacobite lines was a stone wall, stretching down towards the enemy. Before battle had begun, Lord George Murray had asked that it be demolished. He feared that Hanoverian soldiers could creep up behind it and fire on the Jacobite right wing. Unfortunately, there was little willingness, and less time, to comply with his wishes. Now, as the Highlanders charged, Murray was proved tragically right and they were subjected to a punishing volley of shots from Hanoverian troops concealed behind the wall. Another body of Hanoverian cavalry, led by Major Wolfe, charged up to their left, causing further carnage. The Hanoverian infantry immediately in front of them advanced, knelt, fired a volley from their muskets and yet more men fell. Still, the Hanoverian cannons kept firing. They had changed their ammunition from cannonball to grapeshot, which scattered amongst the advancing Highlanders, cutting into their flesh as they ran. In spite of the carnage, those who were not felled charged on into the front lines of Hanoverian infantry, but for all their valour and determination, their cause was clearly hopeless. Those who made it through the front line were caught by the second. There could be precious few survivors.

While the right and the centre charged to their deaths, the left wing of the Highland army was spurred into action by Alexander Macdonald of Keppoch. He was shot as he began to run and a second wound killed him before he reached the enemy lines. His fellow clansmen, seeing the carnage to the right of them, advanced with some hesitancy and were subjected to fire from the front and the side. Before they could reach the Hanoverians opposite them, it became clear that defeat was inevitable and they fled.

The regiments in the second line of the Jacobite army never fully engaged in the battle. The left wing played a valiant role in defending the Macdonalds as they retreated back towards them, pursued by English dragoons, but within a short space of time the English army was advancing en masse towards them and retreat was the only realistic option. After the initial prolonged cannonade, there had been little more than ten minutes of active fighting, the battle was over and the Jacobite army had been devastated. Prince Charles, watching in speechless horror as his men were slaughtered, was persuaded with difficulty to leave the field, accompanied by Lord Elcho, O' Sullivan, and a small body of men.

The fugitives of the Jacobite army were chased from the field by English dragoons. Some of the survivors fled to Inverness, whilst others, including the prince's party, headed for the River Nairn, made their way across and from there dispersed into the hills. Many

of the first group did not make it as far as Inverness. They were
pursued by English horsemen who had no difficulty in catching
up with them. Cumberland had ordered that no quarter should
be given and, accordingly, those that were caught, including
women and children who had travelled with the army, were killed.
The killings continued when the English soldiers reached the town.
According to the sources, some of those killed were not in the
Jacobite army, but were citizens of Inverness who had come to view
the battle and had been caught up in the retreat. The number of those
killed in flight is thought to have been more than 1000.

Hundreds of men lay dead and dying on the battlefield.
Comparatively few of them were Hanoverian soldiers. Whilst the
Jacobites had seen so many of their army fall, either dead or
wounded, the casualties in Cumberland's army were much lighter,
amounting to approximately 250 wounded and less than 100 killed.
The wounded on the battlefield were shown no mercy. On the
orders of General Hawley and the duke himself, they were system-
atically killed by Hanoverian soldiers who patrolled the battlefield,
searching for signs of life among the men who lay there.

There were prisoners taken, but they were treated with appalling
barbarity. They were held captive, scarcely clad or naked and semi-
starved in the tolbooth at Inverness, from where they were eventually taken, put aboard ships and shipped to London. Only a small
proportion of them survived the journey. Some of those taken captive after Culloden were found to have defected to the prince's side
from the government army. They were swiftly tried and executed.

Cumberland's contempt for the Jacobites and his cruel nature
had already been made manifest long before the battle of Culloden.
In his progress from Perth to Aberdeen, he had subjected people in
neighbourhoods sympathetic to the Jacobite cause to merciless
reprisals. People had been burned out of their homes. Suspected
spies had been summarily executed. But after Culloden the behav-
iour of his troops, acting on his command, was exceptionally bar-
baric. In an attempt to justify his actions, Cumberland produced a
document, which he said had come into his possession from enemy
hands, and which was supposedly written and signed by Lord

George Murray. The document was a regimental order, which gave instructions to the Jacobite army that no quarter should be given. Whether Cumberland believed that this document was genuine or not is uncertain. The document was almost certainly a fake. But Cumberland did use it as enticement to his officers to exact the cruellest of revenge and as justification when they followed his orders. His actions earned him an unenviable nickname – 'the Butcher'.

CHAPTER FORTY-TWO

The Flight

It had only taken one defeat, after a remarkable run of victories, to extinguish Jacobite hopes for the success of the '45 rebellion. Ironically, of all the battles fought by the prince's army, it was the one that they had had the most time to plan. The list of 'what-ifs' is a long one. What if they had concentrated their forces along the banks of the Spey instead of distributing them so widely over the north of Scotland in March? Could they have defeated Cumberland as he attempted to cross? What if they had fought on Murray's chosen battlefield instead of Drumossie Moor? Would Cumberland have passed them and taken Inverness, or would he have come to battle? If he did come to battle, would he have won? What if the army had pursued Hawley's men to Edinburgh after the battle of Falkirk and taken the capital?

The 'what-ifs' get us nowhere. In reality, the extent of the success that the prince had in his daring enterprise was astonishing, but the odds against him achieving his aim were probably insurmountable. The longer he campaigned, whether in Scotland or in England, the more time the government had to gather the resources to oppose him. The huge support which the prince never failed to give up hoping for was never forthcoming. There were far fewer supporters of the Jacobite cause than he had anticipated, both in England and in Scotland. Amongst those who might offer their support in word, particularly in England, there were far fewer who were prepared to offer it in deed. From the very beginning, his army was handicapped by lack of arms, men and crucially, money. Help was sent from France, and money was sent from Spain, but not all of it reached the prince's army. It happened that the defeat took place at Culloden, but if it had not happened there, in all likelihood, it would have happened somewhere else.

Lord George Murray and the remnants of the Jacobite army that had fled in the same direction made their way over the hills, keeping well hidden for fear of capture by Hanoverian soldiers, and gathered together eventually at Ruthven Barracks where the prince had told them to wait. The day after the battle, Lord George Murray wrote to the prince from Ruthven, resigning his command. The letter was highly critical of certain aspects of the campaign. Murray stated that the standard should never have been raised without positive reassurances of substantial aid from France. With regard to the military commanders selected by Charles, Murray was particularly scathing about O'Sullivan's incompetence. In spite of Murray's resignation, there was hope among the chiefs who had gathered at Ruthven that there would be a rallying and plans would be made to continue the rebellion. Only two days after the battle, there were more than 2000 men at Ruthven. But their hopes were short-lived. It was only a matter of days before a message was relayed from the prince that the men were to disperse to their own homes with due regard for their personal safety. Reluctantly, the men at Ruthven took their leave of one another and went their separate ways.

Whether the prince had ever had any intention of resuming the campaign in Scotland is uncertain, but if he did, it is likely that Murray's resignation helped to make up his mind for him. Although he had been terribly defeated at Culloden, Charles was confident that the success the Jacobite army had enjoyed up until that point would be enough to convince the French king that another attempt at rebellion, if properly funded and backed with French military power, could succeed. There was nothing to be gained, and much to be lost, if he remained in Scotland. If he returned to France, he believed he would be able use his powers of persuasion to get substantial help from Louis for a return to Scotland. Then, perhaps, he would succeed in reclaiming the throne for the Stewarts.

Chapter Forty-Three

The Aftermath of Culloden

Following the battle at Culloden, Cumberland embarked upon what can only be described as a reign of terror in the Highlands. From his base at Fort Augustus, he sent out his men to scour the countryside in search of Jacobite soldiers and sympathisers. He was determined to stamp out every atom of resistance in these rebellious regions. The homes and estates of Jacobite leaders were plundered and destroyed. Cattle were driven away and families turned out of their homes. The cruelties of Cumberland's men were often indiscriminate. There were shootings and house burnings, imprisonments, thefts and rape. There was little regard shown for real justice. Cumberland was after revenge. He remained in Scotland for nearly three months, his troops leaving a trail of devastation and despair in their wake.

In the light of the terrible reprisals that the people of the Highlands were suffering, it is all the more surprising that the prince was never given up to the Hanoverian troops. They combed the countryside in search of him, frequently coming dangerously close, but no one gave up the secret of where he was hiding, in spite of the risk to their own lives.

CHAPTER FORTY-FOUR

Five Long Months

From Culloden field, the prince had been led across the River Nairn four miles to the southwest of the battlefield. The party followed the course of the river upstream for a distance before turning west to the Great Glen, heading in the direction of Fort Augustus.

At four o'clock in the morning the prince's party arrived at Invergarry Castle. The castle was unoccupied and unfurnished, and the prince and his men fell into an exhausted sleep on the floor. When they woke the next day, they breakfasted on salmon caught from the River Garry. In the early afternoon, the prince left Invergarry, accompanied only by O'Sullivan, Edward Burke, who had guided the party away from the battlefield and Captain O'Neill. It was the beginning of a long journey for him.

From Invergarry, the group continued their journey down the Great Glen towards the southern end of Loch Arkaig. They turned west along the shore of Loch Arkaig and late in the evening arrived at the house of Donald Cameron of Glenpean, where they spent the night. The next day, they continued westwards, and spent the night of 18 April in a farmhouse at Meoble. From Meoble, they travelled to Loch Morar, where they found shelter in a shepherd's hut. The first part of their journey had been made on horseback, but now they were on foot, having been forced to leave their mounts at Meoble because of the difficulty of the terrain.

The next part of their journey took them across the mountainous district of South Morar to Glen Beasdale, near Arisaig. It was from Glen Beasdale that the prince wrote to Murray, informing him of his intention to leave for France. Here, they were joined by a number of others who were in flight after Culloden, including the young Clanranald and Aeneas Macdonald, and they discussed how the prince might safely be got out of the country. There were government ships constantly patrolling the western coastline and it was clear that an escape by sea at this point would be impossible. The prince had to be kept safely in hiding until such time as it was safe for him to sail. Charles hoped for help from Alexander Macdonald of Boisdale, or the laird of Macleod, but was assured that to ask them for help was dangerous. In the end, it was decided that he could find a safe place to stay of Benbecula and, on the evening of 24 April, the prince and seven others put out to sea from Loch nan Uamh.

The distance from Morar to Benbecula, as the crow flies, is more than 70 miles. Travelling this distance in a small boat requires both skill and endurance, even when the seas are calm. When the royal party reached open water, they soon realised that their journey was going to be even more difficult, as a terrible storm had blown up. It was nothing short of a miracle that they reached their destination approximately ten hours later without mishap. They put ashore at Roisinis and found themselves shelter in a semi-derelict cow-house. They stayed on Benbecula for three days, then set out to sea again, in a northerly direction. They hoped to reach Stornoway on the island of Lewis, but once again, the weather turned stormy and they were driven ashore on the island of Scalpay, halfway towards their destination. Most of the inhabitants of the island were anti-Jacobite and the prince's party only escaped detection by pretending they were merchants from Orkney who had been shipwrecked. They found an islander who was willing to lend them a boat, and sent Donald Macleod, who had acted as pilot on the journey from Morar, ahead to Stornoway, to find out whether a vessel could be hired from there to take the prince to France. On 3 May, news was relayed back to them that a vessel had been procured. Charles set sail for Stornoway in another borrowed boat, reaching it on the afternoon of 5 May. Donald Macleod found them a place to stay at Kildun while final preparations were made for the prince's departure.

Misfortune struck again. Word had got out that the vessel was for the use of the prince and the captain, fearing for his life, refused to take him. The little party put out to sea again on 10 May, returning south to Scalpay. They were on the point of making a landing when they realised that people were waiting ashore to capture them and hastily put out to sea again. The journey was fraught with danger. There were English ships patrolling the waters between Skye and Harris and one of them was soon in pursuit of the prince's boat. Fortunately for the royal party, their small sailing boat was faster and more manoeuvrable than the English man-of-war. Having successfully outrun it, they headed for Benbecula and landed on the shores of Loch Uisgebhagh on the west coast. They found a ramshackle hut in which to sleep and made is as comfortable as they could. A message was sent to the old laird of Clanranald who lived on the island, asking for supplies, and the old man gladly provided them with food drink and fresh clothes. After a couple of nights on Benbecula, another hiding place was found for the prince and he was moved to South Uist, to a place called Glencorrodale. They had reasonably comfortable living quarters and as it was a relatively remote spot, they felt safe to stay there for a while. The prince occupied himself hunting and fishing for his own food, guarded by attendants provided by Clanranald.

The three weeks that the prince spent at Glencorrodale provided a welcome period of calm and rest, giving him time to recuperate from the strain and deprivations of recent times. All too soon, however, it became clear that Hanoverian troops were closing in on the area and Charles's hiding place was no longer secure. It was time to move on. The next few weeks were spent almost constantly on the move. Their first stop was the tiny island of Wiay, between South Uist and Benbecula, where they stayed four nights. Then they returned to Roisinis for two nights, before spending a night out in the open on South Uist. Their every move was perilous, for government troops were very close at hand. There were ships patrolling the Minch and troops searching the islands for the prince. There was a price of £30,000 on his head, so the soldiers were eager to catch him. Next day, the prince's group moved further down the coast of South Uist and spent another night in the open before being forced to take refuge further inland for a couple of days. It was fortunate for the prince that summer was on its way and the weather was getting warmer. For much of the month of June, as he moved here and there between Benbecula and South Uist, he was without proper shelter and had to sleep in clefts in the rock, caves, or in the open. Towards the end of this time, he took the decision that it was safer for all concerned if he travelled with only one companion, and parted from John O'Sullivan, Donald Macleod, and Edward Burke, taking only O'Neil with him. As the days passed, it seemed as if it would be only a matter of time before Charles would be caught.

It was at this point that Flora Macdonald entered the prince's life. Flora Macdonald's father, who was dead, had been a South Uist man. Flora normally lived on the Isle of Skye with her widowed mother, but had recently been staying with family in South Uist. Her family had strong connections with Clanranald and she gladly agreed to his request that she might help the prince. A plan was proposed for her to take the prince with her to Skye. The journey would not be easy. Somehow, they had to obtain passes for both Flora and Charles to make the journey and keep Charles's identity concealed from the authorities. It was decided that it would cause the least suspicion if Flora were to obtain passes for both herself and a maidservant to make the crossing. Charles would have to be disguised as the maidservant. The necessary documents were obtained. The chosen name for the prince was Betty Burke. 'Betty' was supposed to be Irish, and was travelling to the Macdonald house in Skye with the highest commendations for her work.

On 27 June, Flora Macdonald came to the prince's hiding place on Benbecula, bringing his new clothes to try on. Much to everyone's relief, he remained light-hearted, and was highly amused with his female disguise. The next evening, Charles said goodbye to his remaining companion, O'Neil, and set off from Loch Uisgebhagh to cross over to Skye with Flora Macdonald. Yet again the Scottish weather turned against him. A storm blew up in the second half of the night and it was hard to for the boatmen to get their bearings, but as dawn broke they saw that they were not far from the island. They were heading towards land at Waternish, when their suspicions were aroused by a group of soldiers onshore. Ignoring the soldiers' commands for them to land, they turned back for open water again. They eventually landed at Kilmuir, a little more than ten miles to the north. Flora left the prince waiting nearby while she went to the house of Lady Margaret Macdonald. Lady Margaret's husband was in the service of the duke of Cumberland, but she was sympathetic to the prince's cause and had been kept informed to some extent of his movements. At Lady Margaret's home, Flora managed to enlist the help of Macdonald of Kingsburgh, who was visiting. Macdonald agreed to offer the prince shelter in his own home some miles away. Macdonald and the prince set off to Kingsburgh on foot. Flora followed shortly after.

The prince slept well that night, enjoying the rare comfort of a proper bed. The next day, Kingsburgh provided him with a fresh set of women's clothes for the next part of the journey, and a suit of man's clothes to change into. Then Kingsburgh, Flora Macdonald, and the prince set off for Portree. When they drew close to Portree, the prince changed into his men's clothes and took his leave of his companions. He spent a night in Portree at an inn in the company of a few loyal men and the next morning was taken in a boat the short distance to the island of Raasay. There was no safe haven for him there, however. The island had been devastated by the military and all the houses had been burned to the ground. The men who had brought him over to the island could only find a ramshackle shepherd's hut for him to rest in. The people of the island were loyal, and the soldiers had gone, but the prince soon became restless. After a couple of nights on the island, he returned in the same boat to Skye, landing at Scorobreck on Trotternish. They found shelter in a byre and settled down for another night. The next day, the prince walked some thirty miles to Elgol with a man called Malcolm Macleod. After an exhausting journey, they met up with members of the Mackinnon clan and were offered lodgings for the night. The next day, after much debate, it was decided that the prince should be taken back to the mainland. He set off that night, accompanied by the laird and a clansman called John Mackinnon. They landed, at four in the morning on 5 July, in North Morar, not far from Mallaig.

The area was crawling with government soldiers and danger was ever present. The prince and his companions slept out in the open for three nights, close to their landing-place, before attempting to move on. On the fourth day, the prince was out on Loch Morar with some of his companions when they were spotted by some soldiers on shore. The soldiers gave chase in their boat and it was only after a prolonged pursuit that the prince and his companions escaped. The next place the party tried to find shelter was with Macdonald of Morar. After making their way through the hours if darkness to Macdonald's house, they discovered that it had been burned to the ground. Macdonald and his family were sheltering in a bothy nearby. In spite of their own difficulties, Macdonald and his wife provided the party with food and then showed them to a cave where they could spend the night. The next day, the prince took his leave of the elderly laird of Mackinnon and continued his journey with John Mackinnon. They went to Borrodale, to the house of Angus Macdonald where the prince had first stayed when he landed from France. When they reached there, the same sort of sight greeted them as at Morar. Macdonald's house had been destroyed by Hanoverian troops. John Mackinnon now left the prince, and Macdonald of Borrodale found him shelter for a few nights in a hut nearby. From there he was moved to another place, four miles to the east on the coast, where a rough shelter had been constructed in a cleft in the rock. This was to be his home for another few days, until once again, it became too dangerous for him to stay any longer. After a night in Glen Morar, the prince received information that government troops were virtually all around him. The decision was taken to move over the mountains.

The prince's companions for this journey were Glenaladale, who had joined the prince at Borrodale, his brother, John Macdonald, and another John Macdonald, son of Angus of Borrodale. The next three nights were spent in the open, the prince and his companions ever conscious of the presence of enemy soldiers. At night, the campfires of the military were visible for miles around. They climbed Sgurr Thuilm then descended into Glen Pean, where they were joined by Donald Cameron of Glen Pean. Then they climbed

again towards Loch Quoich, and bypassing its western edge, continued north to Kinloch Hourn. The journey was exhausting, but
they kept up a steady pace. The last stage of their journey took them
over the high ground south of Glenshiel. On the third day, they
arrived in Glenshiel. It was the third week in July. The prince had
been on the run for three months.

Glenshiel was Mackenzie territory. Although the party knew they
could trust no one here and still had to keep their presence well
concealed, they were no longer in danger from patrolling soldiers.
Donald Cameron left them here, and they continued down
Glenshiel to Loch Clunie, then climbed some way up Sgurr nan
Conbhairean, to the north of the loch. It was 28 July. After spending
an uncomfortable night in a tiny cave on the hillside, the prince's
party learned that there was a group of seven veterans of Culloden
living rough in the area. They were staunch Jacobites who had
taken an oath between them never to give up their arms. These
men were living on their wits, stealing whatever they could from
groups of Hanoverian soldiers in order to survive. Their daring
exploits had already given them quite a fearsome reputation. It was
decided that the prince would be as safe with these men as he
would with any others and accordingly, Glenaladale's brother was
sent to find them. The names of the seven men were Patrick Grant
(Black Peter of Craskie), John Macdonnell or Campbell, Alexander
Macdonnell, the Chisholm brothers, Alexander, Donald and Hugh,
and Grigor Macgregor.

The 'Seven Men of Glenmoriston' were found and without
knowing that the prince was in the group, agreed to take the fugitives in. When they met up with the rest of the group, they recognised Charles at once. The prince and his companions were treated
with the greatest courtesy and kindness. For three nights they
stayed in one cave, before moving to another one a short distance
away for another four nights. The week spent with the Seven Men
of Glenmoriston did much to restore the prince's spirits. Their loyalty was unquestionable and their kindness towards him, ensuring
that he had every possible comfort they could afford him, could not

have been greater. On 6 August, it was time to move on again. There were Campbell soldiers in the area.

The seven men accompanied the prince on the next part of his journey. Their next destination was Strathglass, and they stayed in this area until 13 August, awaiting news from a messenger who had been sent to Poolewe to find out whether there were any French ships off the coast there. The news came back that there had been a French ship there, but it had left. Some of its crew had been left behind to search for the prince and they were looking for him between Loch Eil and Loch Arkaig.

The prince and his party set out on the journey south again. It took two days for the party to reach Loch Arkaig. They stayed in the vicinity for almost two weeks. During this time, the prince managed to make contact by messenger with Cameron of Lochiel and Cluny MacPherson, and decided to move further east to join them.

The reunion with Lochiel took place in Lochiel's hideout close to Ben Alder. Lochiel had been badly wounded at Culloden and although he was much recovered, still had great difficulty walking on account of his injuries. A couple of days later, Cluny MacPherson arrived and led the prince and Lochiel to what was to be their final place of residence on Scottish soil. Cluny had constructed a remarkable hiding place on the slopes of Ben Alder – a two-storey affair, making use of natural features in the rocky landscape with the addition of turf, logs and branches to provide protection from the elements and a degree of comfort for its inhabitants. It was the perfect hideout – well camouflaged from the outside, it nonetheless afforded the fugitives a panoramic view of the countryside round about. Charles and Lochiel stayed here with Cluny for over a week in relative comfort. At last the news they had been longing for was brought to them. Two French ships, *L'Hereux* and *Le Prince de Conti,* had arrived in the waters off the west coast of Scotland and had managed to put ashore at Loch nan Uamh. The prince and Lochiel set off at once. The journey was made with all haste and considerable anxiety, in case the French ships were forced to leave Scottish shores before they could reach them. On 19 September, seven days after leaving Ben Alder, Prince Charles's party reached Loch nan Uamh. Late that night, he and Lochiel boarded *L'Heureux*. Under cover of darkness, the two ships made their way out to sea, taking the prince back to France.

> *Bonny Charlie's noo awa',*
> *Safely o'er the friendly main.*
> *Moany a heart will break in twa,*
> *Should he no' come back again.*

> *Will ye no' come back again?*
> *Will ye no' come back again?*
> *Better lo'ed ye canna be,*
> *Will ye no' come back again?*

CHAPTER FORTY-FIVE

Prisoners and Fugitives

The atrocities committed by Cumberland's men in the weeks immediately after the battle of Culloden included the summary executions of countless fugitives. From July 1746, the trials of those who had been taken capture during and after the '45 rebellion began. Seventeen men from the Manchester regiment that was captured at Carlisle were taken to London for trial at the end of July, found guilty and condemned to death. Nine of them were hung, drawn and quartered the day after sentencing. The other eight were reprieved for three weeks before sentence was carried out. Three of the Scottish troops who had been captured at Carlisle suffered a similar fate some weeks later. All of the other prisoners who had been captured at various times during the campaign were brought to England for trials in the months that followed. Almost 400 men were herded into prison at Carlisle. On the Thames, prison ships kept many hundreds more confined in cramped squalid conditions. The fort at Tilbury was also filled with captives. Most of the officers had to face trial. A lottery system was used to decide which of the rank and file should face trial and which should be transported to the colonies. One in twenty was tried. The fate of the large majority who were tried and found guilty was ultimately transportation; almost 1000 men were transported; 91 men were sentenced to death at Carlisle, and another 70 at York. Although a significant number of those who received the death sentence at Carlisle or York were ultimately reprieved, approximately 80 prisoners had been executed by mid-November.

Several members of the Scottish nobility who had supported Charles were also brought to trial. The earl of Kilmarnock and Lord Balmerino were found guilty and beheaded. The earl of Cromarty was given a reprieve. Charles Radcliffe, earl of Derwentwater, and brother of the earl of Derwentwater who had been beheaded after the rebellion of 1715, was captured on board a French supply ship bound for Scotland in 1745. Like his brother, he had been sentenced to death in 1716 for his part in the rising, but he had escaped from Newgate prison. There was no need for a second trial. He appeared in court and the sentence that had been delivered 30 years previously was read out to him again. He was executed in December 1746. Murray of Broughton, the Prince's secretary, was captured after Culloden in the Borders and sent to London. There, he saved his own life by turning king's evidence against a number of others, including the elderly Simon Fraser, Lord Lovat. Lord Lovat's commitment to the cause of the House of Stewart had wavered throughout earlier campaigns and intrigues, but during the rebellion of 1745, he finally came out for the prince. He suffered the ultimate penalty for his untimely decision to side with the Jacobites. He was captured some weeks after the battle of Culloden, hiding in a hollowed-out tree in the middle of Loch Morar. He was taken to London for trial and, in March 1747, was beheaded.

Flora Macdonald had been captured shortly after leaving the prince at Portree on the Isle of Skye. From Skye she was sent to Leith, near Edinburgh, where she spent some months imprisoned on a troopship, before being sent to London. She was eventually released from captivity and returned to Skye, where she married the son of Macdonald of Kingsburgh. They emigrated to America, but seven years before her death in 1790, returned to Skye. Captain O'Neill, who had accompanied the prince during his flight until Charles left for Skye, was captured and sent to London. His fate after that is not known. Edward Burke and O'Sullivan escaped on a boat bound for France.

The laird of Mackinnon and John Mackinnon, who had travelled with Charles from Skye to the mainland, were both captured by government troops shortly after they each took their separate leave of him. Both men were taken by ship to London, but were eventually released in 1747.

A number of others who played a part in the prince's escape were subsequently taken prisoner, including MacLeod, the boatman, and Malcolm Macleod, who had walked to Elgol with Charles.

Cluny MacPherson remained in hiding for several years after the rebellion, always hopeful that the prince would return.

Several of the men of high rank in the prince's army made good their escape from Scotland before Charles. They included the duke of Perth, Lord Elcho and Lord John Drummond, who fled on French ships from the west coast. Lord George Murray also escaped, by a more difficult route. He died in Holland 14 years later.

CHAPTER FORTY-SIX

Consequences

It was from the Highlands that the greatest support for the most troublesome of the Jacobite rebellions had come. Consequently, it was in the Highlands that the harshest effects of the government's determination to stamp out the threat of further risings were felt the most. Cumberland's ferocious reprisals against the Jacobite chiefs and their clans were only the beginning. The measures carried out by the government were to change the Highlands permanently. When the rising was over, the estates of approximately 40 Jacobite leaders who had been attainted for treason were forfeited to the Crown. Plans were made for the fortification and garrisoning of the Highlands, building on the work that General Wade had begun after 1719. Construction began on a new Fort George, while Fort William and Fort Augustus were rebuilt and a number of other fortified properties were adapted for the use of occupying garrisons. The network of military roads was greatly extended.

In 1746, the government passed another Disarming Act and this time it was enforced with sanctions. Those who were found in possession of weapons in contravention of the act were imprisoned. Second offenders were transported. The same act also banned the wearing of tartan and of any part of traditional Highland dress.

The Disarming Act was humiliating, but the second act passed by the government was devastating. This act abolished heritable jurisdictions, removing the hereditary rights of landowners in Scotland to exercise the law and dispense justice to their tenants. More importantly, the act removed the hereditary power of wardholding, which had always been exercised by the Highland chiefs, obliging their clansmen to be available for military service in return for protection and land. By removing the power of the chiefs to summon their men to battle, the government was ensuring that never again could a Highland army be raised against them. But the act also effectively destroyed the structure of the clan system. The chief, once a patriarchal ruler, lawgiver and military leader, whose power depended on the number of clansmen he could maintain on his lands, became a mere landlord, dependent on cash income for his living. His clansmen, once soldiers and loyal followers, became tenants.

The Episcopalian Church, whose members had provided so much support for the Jacobites, also felt the weight of the government's displeasure. Laws were passed that restricted the activities of both parishioners and clergy. All Episcopalian ministers were made to take oaths of allegiance to George II, and the king's name was to be mentioned in prayers at meetings of worship. Episcopalians could not meet for worship in groups of more than five people and their services had to be led by someone who had taken the oath of allegiance. Failure to comply with these laws could result in imprisonment.

CHAPTER FORTY-SEVEN

The End of Bonnie Prince Charlie

The government in Britain had made sure that a rebellion on anything like the scale of the '45 could never happen again. Prince Charles had left Scotland full of hope for support from Louis XV for a comeback, but sadly, he was to be disappointed. Louis gave him a warm enough welcome in France, but would not contemplate the idea of funding another expedition. In 1748, much against his will, the prince was forced to leave France, as part of France's commitment to Great Britain under the terms of the Treaty of Aix-La-Chapelle. He moved from France to Avignon and then for a number of years, led a fairly nomadic existence around Europe. In Great Britain, committed Jacobites continued plotting. In 1750, it is claimed that Charles visited London, hoping to play a part in a plot to overthrow the House of Hanover. In 1753, another Jacobite plot was hatched in England and Scotland and the prince voiced his interest again, but the plans came to nothing.

Charles's life began to disintegrate. His relationship with Clementina Walkinshaw, whom he had met in Scotland in 1745, was resumed in Europe, but ended very bitterly after seven years. In 1766, his father died. True Jacobites might recognise Charles as king now, but, to his great disappointment, the pope refused. Charles's marriage in 1772 to Princess Louisa of Stolberg was brief, unhappy and violent. Charles was an embittered alcoholic. He spent the final years of his life as an invalid, tended by his daughter Charlotte. On 31 January 1788, Charles died. The Jacobite cause had died some time before him.